One Man's GOLD

Joan Baxter

Michael Terence Publishing

First published in paperback by
Michael Terence Publishing in 2018
www.mtp.agency

ISBN 9781912639564

A CIP record for this publication
may be found with the British Library

*With thanks to Thame Library staff for their untiring
and ever-friendly help.*

One Man's
GOLD

Joan Baxter

Contents

The Sourdough

An icy blast drove Jed further into his jacket. He had 'Alaskan' chiselled into his face, and the wind cutting across Cook Inlet carved it even deeper.

Every winter Jed asked himself why he stayed. California, that was the place. Move with the sun. But he never did.

Jed pulled into a doorway for shelter. He should have gone to the mission and got some good hot soup inside him, but he hadn't done that either. Jed didn't seem to want to do anything any more.

Becoming aware of his surroundings, he saw he had stopped at a pawnshop. Jed felt a sudden empathy with the objects in the window. They stood for something that belonged to the past; to something that might have been.

Bits of jade, ivory, old coins, the odd gold nugget or two spilling from a dried out poke. Those were the days alright. Full of hope he'd been then. How many centuries ago was that he wondered. He and the boys had worked a placer mine then on Deadman's Creek. Where were they now, the old crowd, Mike, Benny, Phil, Chuck, and the rest? He remembered the long winter they'd spent snowed up in the cabin with nothing to do but wait for summer. And when it came, they worked almost twenty-four hours a day under the midnight sun.

And Rose; always good for a song and a laugh. Heart of gold had Rose and a voice like a fog-horn. Taverns were taverns then. It didn't matter Rose couldn't sing; she could be just about anything to any man. Everyone loved her, though Jed had hoped…but she'd always held back. Some said she'd been given a bad time in the past, but who could know.

Jed had promised her the first nugget that came out of their claim. He'd given it to her in a brand new poke and told her there was more where that came from. What a celebration there'd been that night in the saloon. Drinks all round and don't spare the fiddler. Jed had played his squeezebox while Rose sang; Dan stood on the table and did a tap-dance and played the spoons. At midnight it was like New Year's Eve as everyone went into the street and fired into the air. Wasn't every day someone struck it rich and they were still whooping it up next day.

Then came the blow; when they went to market the stuff. Dumping the poke on the counter, they could hardly wait. Then: 'Pyrite' they were told, 'Fools Gold'.

After that, Jed knocked around the lower 48[1], riding the freight trains and looking for an easy

---

[1] Lower 48 States as expressed by Alaskans

buck. He had even roped steers at the Rodeo, though that was no easy buck! But the Big Country called and before long Jed was back, determined to make good this time. Oh yes, he was going to make a fortune. Hah! With gold at a stable $35. per oz. why not?

It was stable alright. As costs rose, the price of gold stuck. Everyone else was in the same spot so Jed couldn't even sell the equipment. Ghosts of dredgers, sluice channels, even a few cabins still remained – grave-yards of one-time boom towns.

For Jed there followed a round of logging camps, work in a sawmill, on fishing trawlers, tramp ships and husky mail runs. He had even worked a trap-line with an Athabascan Indian. But nothing lasted and he learned a man can get lonely by himself in a long winter.

Today it was gold, black gold, liquid gold. There was money on the north slopes alright and the youngsters thought it was all new. He had given it a try with 'em and after three months on the offshore platforms the kids were at each other's throats. Ha, they shoulda been with him and boys that winter in the cabin on Deadman's Creek. He could teach 'em a thing or two about living. What was oil to a Sourdough?[2]

Jed's eyes came back to the window and fluttered

---

[2] Old-timers who relied on sourdough to leaven their bread when shacked up for winter with no fresh supplies. Piece of dough left from previous batch

over a dusty squeezebox. He wondered where his own lay rotting. He went in. Yes, it was for sale but not at a price Jed could afford. He wiped his hand across his mouth, flexed his stiff fingers and asked if he might try it. The music brought people into the shop. All they heard these days was the jukebox, sometimes a guitar, but nothing was spontaneous any more. People liked it; some even gave him money.

'Tell ya what' said the pawnbroker, with an eye to business 'You can come in here any time and play that thing. You can give me what you get. That way we'll both be happy'.

But before the accordion was completely his, Jed was being asked to play for local hops, at the sawdust and peanut replicas of old days, prettied up for tourists. Jed was happy. He didn't have gold or oil, but he had a squeezebox again, contentment, friends and his memories. Not that there wasn't still the occasional brawl but time was when it wasn't a night out without a good punch-up. He'd known the place when it was a tent town. Things had got tame since then but it suited his years. Even women weren't the same. He chuckled, but that suited him too.

There were a few old sourdoughs like himself who still managed to pan a living from the hills, coming into the city only to sell the stuff. And there were those who earned more by panning as a tourist attraction along with selling pots of sourdough.

Jed looked round at the people he was playing to, and knew that for the first time in his life, he was really rich; for he had something they could never have. He had known the real thing, he had been there, seen men kill and be killed. They could never know, and were content to sit on the sidelines and enjoy a tame reproduction. Where were they now those real people? He knew it was only in his head but as he played, so a foghorn voice rang out, loud and lusty. He listened, terrified that someone might spoil the illusion before it faded. But it didn't fade, it grew and came close, till it was right there beside him. He couldn't look.

Then the lady at his side took something from her neck and hung it round Jed's neck, leaving the stone resting in her large, worn hand. He knew what it was without looking. The nugget he'd given to Rose oh – centuries ago. It wasn't gold, but she had kept it, worn it, and that made it gold enough for Jed; and all the gold he'd ever want.

The Presidential Chef

Leonardo, ex-presidential chef, must be the only man in Alaska who wasn't there to make his fortune. He was there for more unique reasons – pressing reasons. But our paths had yet to be crossed. And there was quite a bit of in between to be covered before they did.

Anchorage was simply laid out at the feet of the Chugach Mountains, to the East. Across Knik Arm to the West the Alaska Range stood behind Mt. Susitna, the Sleeping Lady. Naked white she glowed flimsy pink in the sun's first and last peep of the day. I looked around me, and saw yesterday etched into the faces that slouched passed or limply loitered. Some had seen and done it all but couldn't give up. Some did nothing and never would. This was not the same yesterday that I had dropped into, by crossing the date line, to arrive literally in yesterday's night before, but a yesterday that had sculpted itself deeply through the time of yesteryears.

Just coming to Alaska on 'spec' was a gamble and I was amazed at how some of them still did. One old-timer played a concertina he'd won in a dice game; another had lost a gold mine in a card game (when gold had more value than it did today). Taking a chance seemed to be part of the quest, and the taller the story, the more likely it proved to be true.

A trapper was talking to me about his mother-in-law who had a tattooed chin, which he said showed she was a high-born Eskimo. Her husband, who did unexplained things like burning paper without fire was, appropriately, an Eskimo Chief. A bush plane parked in a car-park, looked out of place for a mere second or two, then appeared perfectly normal, reasonable; more so when I attempted to fulfil my romantic notion of getting to Nome by dog sled. Air travel was much cheaper, no need to supply food for the dogs, myself or the team leader. It was also quicker. I reluctantly gave in to flight. From Nome to my destination of Lost River should be no trouble.

Airborne across the Kuskakwim River the land below was flat and lonely. Mt. Mckinley, stood content that she was the loftiest head on the North American continent. On the other side, the Kuskakwims were a nest of beauties; ice rivers scored dark divisions between the peaks.

Further, there was absolutely nothing below but unblemished virgin snow. The pilot knew differently. He flew low and tossed out some empty drums. No marker in the vastness of white but it must have been the backyard of a snow-hidden house. People instantly appeared, relieving the fierceness of white; smiling and waving up to us, as we circled and lifted.

The Arctic Circle cut through Kotzebue Sound on the Seward Peninsula: when we crossed it, we were over the tundra; the snow was way behind us. The names of Jack London and Robert Service were joined by those of Baron von Kotzebue and William Henry Seward. When Seward bought Alaska from Russia, despite its low cost, he was ridiculed for buying a barren, useless piece of land, which subsequently became known as Seward's Folly. But when its hidden resources were discovered below its face, did the Russians I wonder, rename it a Russian Folly for selling so cheaply?

The Bering Sea was misty grey, the sky was grey and the stone and slate beach was grey. It was a grey daylight.

At the northernmost point of Barrow, greyness had set in thick and vast. I could see nothing, not even a scrap of sea, yet I was looking directly across to the point of the north pole. There was no more north. It had run out. Fly over the pole and we would still be going south. Instead, we turned and flew south on this side of the globe, like a migratory bird.

With a stop-off at Kotzebue we arrived in Nome. Nome received its present name due to a misread 'Name?' on a map in progress. Like so many names where first-timers pitched their tent, and called it home, it stuck. An Alaskan map tells its own story in place names: Big Hurrah, Liven Good, Hard Luck Creek, Soughdough, Chicken, the latter said to have come about through the frustration of the claimant at trying to spell Ptarmigan. Though Grouse might have been more appropriate!

My destination was a placer mine at Lost River. Teller was the next leg of the journey and I asked around. Nome Liquor Store was worth a return visit. It was still busy, though people came to chat as often as they came to buy. A happily oiled Eskimo bought a bottle from the big fair man behind the counter, filled his own jug and drank from a can. He handed 'the Boss' a roll of notes.

'For more when I come back'

'No. No more liquor. Not good'. The customer waved it back

'Alright – here' said the Boss, putting it in an envelope in the till, 'But for plane fare to see Doctor'.

The banning of alcohol was said to be the one thing crooks and clergy agreed upon, even though it was for vastly different reasons.

There was still no-one going to Teller but I could park my pack behind the couch in the back while looking; which was how I unofficially moved into the liquor store. It was a tribute to the Nomite that all I needed each day was toothbrush and money. The church, hospital and personal sofas were all offered as home. The Alaskan was independent, dependable and interdependent.

Nearby Port Safety was just a ferry platform. Inland, abandoned cabins and mining equipment testified to the rising cost of labour and the static price of raw gold at $35 an ounce since 1935. Most working mines now extracted minerals other than gold for that reason.

With still no lift to Teller I helped out with odd jobs, from letter answering to fetching coffee. One of the Boss's colleagues had started a business in artefacts, of which he and the Boss had plenty from their own prospecting days and he needed help with letters. Not for sale was the Boss's own collection of guns: impressive and ornate, pearl handled, bone-handled, modest, filigreed, and all lovingly kept in good condition.

Orders were an education. One letter which asked for an 'oosuk' 14-16 inches long curiosity bade me ask about. It was explained to me so genteelly I could almost believe it, only I didn't.

I was told that an elderly unmarried lady had asked the same question, and when given the same answer, she smiled and said she hoped when she was reincarnated she would come back as a walrus, adding with a twinkle – a *lady* walrus.

I still didn't believe it. The penis bone of a walrus? But like most tall stories in Alaska, it proved to be true. Though to mammal experts it was known as 'bacala' rather than 'oosuk'. Ah well! I was beginning to realise that in Alaska what appeared to be 'tall', including the people, was the norm, suggesting that my thirst for knowledge could be dangerous by leaving me wide open to...the truth!

Getting a flask of coffee sounded far less hazardous. Wrong. Why? This was the point at which our paths crossed – I refer of course to the exceptional Leonardo. Leonardo, the Presidential Chef was in full flow, energetically reliving the previous day's high point. Noted for his reindeer steaks the size of doormats, Leonard, as he was usually known, fed the construction crews. The company paid by arrangement, so when a foreman complained there was a stranger at the table and no other foreman knew him –

'O.K. so this is a bum. When he finish he get up and walk out. O.K. wise guy I say, you like the food o.k. you pay the money o.k. What money? he leers, a big greasy one y'know. He move off. I grab his arm, he grab me, we start'

Leonard went through his ordeal blow for blow, chef's hat quivering frenziedly. Customers were galvanised but with reflexes tuned. Anyone within arms reach was in danger of adding to Nome's collection of black eyes. Leonard's portrayal was thorough.

'Finally I pin him and bang, bang, bang his head, hoping to hear the magic words 'OK I pay' But what happen? It's me who stop. I run out of bang. Leonardo I say to myself, why you should do all the work and he just stand there. I think of my heart and decide to finish this big greasy one. I grab his collar, spin him around and hit him back to the counter, with a right, and a left, and a right. I step back to let him fall down – and still the bum stand up. Then I get him down and quick on top and bang, bang, bang till I hear the magic words, 'OK, I pay'. I get up a happy man. He give me five dollars and then whut!? He insulta me. Big as you like he say 'Keep the change' and walk out'.

Exhausted after his replay fight Leonard sank back in his chair panting and patting his heart.

'And to think I could have stayed in Venezuela and been shot' he wailed, as if it was a preferred choice right now.

A few regulars, feeling it safe to move thought Leonard might like *them* to pay before leaving. Leonard wasn't stirring. He was 'Out'.

'How should I know how much? YOU ate the food' and while Leonard sat fanning himself, customers paid the till, gave themselves change and left.

I gave Leonard cooling space before asking for the coffee.

'Whut you ask me?' Leonard pushed his tall hat round his head.

'You want me to serve you or something? You see where it is', I helped myself and went back to pay. Leonard flounced up as if jabbed with a hot spike, palms flapping like kippers with convulsions. Weak heart? That man had the heart and energy of an ox.

'Whadda you do to me huh? You wanna insult

Leonard? You think this is some cheap coffee shop? I Leonardo should sell coffee now? Take off, take off'.

One thing you can say of the lovable Leonard, he doesn't overcharge.

With a break in my duties, I went with the Boss on a trip out of Nome towards Sullivan City, a grand name for just another neglected gold mine. The vastness stretched to the horizon.

'You wouldn't believe that out there live 2,000 hermits, coming into town once a year only to stock up?'

'No I wouldn't.' Nothing moved, not a sign or sound of life in the entire expanse to the horizon.

The Boss took his .38 revolver from his gun belt and handed it to me. I felt honoured. It was from his collection. A decade ago I had learnt to shoot and not touched a weapon since. It was good to feel a gun in my hand again and was there ever a bigger target range than here? Out of curiosity, a permitted couple of shots into space were clean in the alien silence. Nothing stirred, not even a ptarmigan. When we left, it was like stepping out of a cleansing white enclave we had bathed in. Nothing had touched its purity. But it touched us, and lingered deeply in the cotton wool silence that followed.

Back in Nome, and a short time later, the Boss had a visit from a friend he hadn't seen for a long time. They celebrated their reunion, then decided to take a trip. There was room for me too. They were going to Teller!

The night before leaving we went to eat at Leonard's. Knowing well the size of Leonard's portions, I tentatively asked if he could make me an omelette. Wrong choice of words on my part.

'Can I… can I…Can I Leonardo make…' When Leonard was once more anchored to the floor, he disappeared into the kitchen and in no time appeared with the fluffiest of omelettes. The trouble was, that too was the size of a doormat. Leonard could only think BIG. His template for everything was his doormat sized reindeer steaks. But I had to eat it all as he then sat at our table and watched; something Leonard did when he'd specially prepared a dish or concocted a new sauce. He had to have the customer's response. Delicious of course, but if the customer's reaction was slow to come, he'd lean close, gaze eagerly into his face and urge 'what you think, uh?' Leonard took a pride in his art.

Leonard had indeed been chef to the president of Venezuela, till a coup sent him fleeing for his life, which Leonard had in abundance. Escaping as far away as possible he arrived in Alaska. Leonard had never prospected, staked a claim, or even panned for gold and had no interest in so doing. The rarest of men, he had not come to Alaska to make his fortune. He brought it with him; escaped with it – his life. He was his own treasure and tool to do with it what made him happiest: cheffing. And making your living doing something you enjoy gives life its worth and savour.

There was talk of a travel convention and Leonard was to be given the catering – well who else? Leonard was bursting to talk about it and excitedly showed us the array of dishes - page after page from hors-d'oeuvres to deserts.

'You'll need an army of assistants for this lot' commented one customer.

'No, no, no. Only Leonard in my kitchen. Everybody out, out, out. Anyone in my kitchen make me nervous. Same with figures. I make butter figures and ice figures. Here only ice figures. You gotta be quick, chip, chip, chip and finish. You want to stay long time in the freezer? No'

Leonard was thrilled; brimming with the vision before him. He was Presidential Chef all over again.

Then to celebrate the occasion; with a masterful flourish Leonard produced a large gold nugget and passed it around. Silence dropped awkwardly. Leonard's smile began to shrink.

'Whatsa matter wid you guys?' Still nothing. Then –

'You've been done', said a voice of one who supposed Leonard had bought it.

'Whadaya mean 'done'? Is gold' insisted Leonard

'Looks more like brass'

'Brass you tella me' shrieked Leonard 'You the gold expert?'

'It's not pure gold anyway' said another scratching at it 'Where d'you get it?'

Leonard looked embarrassed. If they weren't going to see the truth, he didn't want to say. They waited. Then:

'Hell, I wasn't gonna take nothing for his meals anyway. He's a good guy'. They still wanted to know who. Leonard looked down. Finally, he looked up with a sigh and said

'Brigadier Holmes of the Salvation Army'

A stunned moment followed then everyone was talking at once 'Yeah, sure – ', 'Gotta be – ', 'Great guy – ', 'Sure thing – ' and so on. Brig. Holmes had been given the nugget thirty years ago when he campaigned at mining camps all over Alaska.

'There's the answer' they decided 'Jangling about with keys and coins for thirty years would do it', 'Sure would make a difference' confirmed another. It was unanimous. It was gold.

Leonard had never doubted it was *pure* gold and always would be. It was recognition of his life's achievements; his survival skills, his artistry and talent, proof that he was still Presidential chef and would be again for the Convention. Nothing could change that, and never would. Nothing!

Specks

En route to the narrow gauge railway that crossed the lower Yukon, the day gained by crossing the International date line was being lassoed back by the hour. Time zones, as well as people and events, whizzed by, making a nonsense of time itself. A candle or sand-timer had more stability. Measuring time by day or night meant little. One day and night of six months each takes care of a year as effectively as 365/6 twenty four hour days. Or a day and night can merge in as little as one or two hours. Time had become a flimsy thing, floating off without substance or meaning. No wonder people say an Eskimo has no idea of time. What is it? And what is it to them? It was ungraspable. I'd certainly lost my grip on it.

Now I was heading south to Alaska's capital, Juneau. When we pulled away from Yukon and White Pass Station it had warmed to -45 F. The Yukon to British Columbia and back into Alaska unravelled a scroll 111 miles long; showing the trail of the Klondike stampede of 1896. The train itself was a bit of history too. It had an iron grid skirt to clear snow and other impedimenta on the line and cried out for a gunfight over its rooftops. Only there was no-one to fight. I had the train to myself. Though as sole passenger I wasn't entirely alone. There was Clancy, a snow clearer and Henry the railroad cook – with no-one to cook for that I could see. We sat round the pot-bellied stove topping each other's tall stories.

Lake Bennet, B.C. a seamless sheet of white, was marked by a lone speck of black, a being reduced to the size of a fly.

'He's jigging' said Clancy. The figure was far from any movement but looked more as if frozen to the spot. Clancy explained,

'He's 'Jigging' for fish through a hole in the ice'. Such patience to 'shop' for a fish dinner.

Over White Pass we were back in Alaska and Dead Horse Gulch, so named for the thousands of pack animals that died here in the Gold Rush days. Further I glimpsed the actual trail, now legendary, travelled today by black gold, oil, carried not by human lines but pipelines.

When we reached Skagway, it looked like being something of an achievement to leave the train.

'No wonder they'd be wanting me down here clearing the snow – it's up here looking in the window', said Clancy, and it was. A pensioned off rotary snow clearer lay by the track. Hopefully, better equipment awaited Clancy, to execute his much-needed skills. I was glad not to be building a boat here, as others were said to have done to reach the gold fields beyond the Yukon River.

Once in Skagway, the first thing that struck me was the wind. It literally knocked the breath out of me and frequent stops in doorways to get it back were necessary. Even when the wind blew behind me, it was hard to believe I was clothed. The temperature was only 18⁰ below but I was learning fast about wind factor.

Understandably, everything was closed and there wasn't a ferry to Juneau for another two days. Help came in the form of Fr. Melbourne. He was going to Haines and invited me to the Catholic Mission for a welcome warm up. News on one of two wood cabinet 'wireless' sets Father liked tinkering with, announced 70 mph winds. Some blast. But when time came for battling the elements, Father got us to Haines where we went our separate ways. Haines ballooned with smooth pillows of snow in a silent sea of white and as Fr. Melbourne disappeared into it, Richard appeared out of it. He too was going to Juneau. Richard had driven to Haines from Anchorage via Tok and like any brave person admitted to being afraid.

'The people at Tok were so good. It was 65⁰ below and they were worried about me going on alone, so I stayed and slept in the warmest place, the pantry.' I could certainly relate to that. Richard continued,

'D'you know they had the snowmobile race through there?' I certainly did. 'That motel had never seen so many people', finished Richard. Having reached Tok myself along with the first 600-mile Snowmobile race, I could well understand that they were still talking about it. My non-heroic role was to bring up the rear in one of the military trucks that followed to pick up stragglers and sort mishaps. But that's another story.

We were looking out to where the ferry should come in. With every attempt, the wind pushed her back, sometimes slamming her into the dock sideways first. She wasn't giving up easily but when it was clear she wasn't going to win this battle, she came in at another dock. Amazingly still in one piece. On this wind, we could have gone by air.

The ferry must have been put together masterfully for she carried us safely, to arrive in the usual dark hours so fondly nurtured by the ferry system.

Juneau huddled like a timid child at the water's edge. Rigid peaks stunted the town's growth yet they suggested guardianship rather than restriction.

Richard had to meet his Boss who had put tracers out for him to check not only where he was but *if* he was, while my quest was somewhere to stay. We arranged to meet the next day to see Juneau.

A hillside guest-house with sweeping views opened its doors. In the office sat white-haired Mrs. J. weighing 90-1bs. and a guest who on his own admission weighed 300-1bs. Not fat. Ralph was as solid in body as he was in character and every ounce a gentleman. A Seventh Day Adventist Mrs. J. enjoyed her daily Bible reading and used my presence to bring out her own hand embroidered cloths for my room.

Ralph was the kind of man who when he accidentally shot himself in the leg, changed his trousers before going to the Doctor to get the bullet removed but didn't mention it to Mrs. J. in case she worried. His kind thought and action might have worked better had he not left his bloodstained, bullet-holed trousers on the floor where Mrs. J. found them. The incident reminded me of someone similar that I had met. An attractive man, despite the lump of metal sticking out of his head - the result of another shooting incident. The skin had grown over it, but he assured me it didn't hurt: it was just too dangerously placed to be removed.

Upstairs, a loose-limbed character was leaning heavily on the door frame. 'I'm Hal' he said. Everything about Hal drooped, his head, his arms, even his fingers hung like long drops of water about to leave their source, but his eyes were alive.

'I live next door' Hal continued, 'Just like to know who I'm living with. Gotta be careful y'know'. Then using an unsure finger as a guideline, after tapping his nose, he looked down it and decided 'You're alright kid, you're alright' then shuffled off. Ambitiously Hal turned and attempted a wink and a wave – at the same time. Hal was pleasant and funny drunk or sober.

From what I'd seen in the short time I'd been here, unless the men were there on a rehabilitation program from the Salvation Army or the SDA Mrs. J. didn't belong in this setting, but they weren't and she did. Ralph was not included in that category. He was a guest who helped Mrs. J. wherever needed.

My aim was a quiet night in; even catch up with some sleep. The sound of the T.V. downstairs, broke into my thoughts when it suddenly stopped. Voices came in gruff jabs and finished with the crashing of furniture. I didn't go down. Ralph was there and that made everything alright.

When it felt right for me to go down, I went. The place was in remarkably good order. Mrs. J. also appeared for the first time. Two State Troopers were already in attendance. Ralph, on hearing the fracas had plunked the offender, who wasn't a border, outside, picked up and cleaned up the man on the wrong end of the fight and put him to bed, cleaned the blood off the floor and walls and replaced the furniture.

Mrs. J. put the kettle on. Ralph dived under Mrs. J's chair.

'Missed those' he said, coming up with two teeth.

Mrs. J. wondered why the intruder had come in the first place.

'Money. He wanted to borrow some' said Ralph. 'The old man didn't have any and that's how it started'. Then turning to me, 'He'll get it hot this time. He's only just come out. You'd think he'd like his freedom'. The offender's record didn't leave out much.

When Mrs. J. brought the tea we discussed next day's arrangements for church. Ralph wasn't SDA but liked the idea of going to church on a Saturday and already had his own children's class.

We chatted into the evening. A few late imbibers returned whom Ralph assisted to lie down. The last of these was Ray, already bleeding from a fall outside. Patched up and standing up Mrs. J. went to him, linked her arm through his, drew herself up to her proudest height and said 'My son'. Her tears came later.

Ray lived in the town. Sometimes Mrs. J. took him home, sometimes it was Ralph. Tonight Ralph walked him back. When Ralph returned he told Mrs. J. all the appreciative things Ray had said about her. Mrs. J. didn't believe him, so Ralph repeated all the things she so delighted in hearing. Tears came quietly. This time, of a different kind.

Next morning I opened the door on an immaculate figure.

'Well I have to have all my suits made. I can't just buy them' explained Ralph. Expensive no doubt, but certainly worth it.

We reached church early so Ralph went to the police station to see 'the guy'. He had looked in earlier on the injured man and still had time for his juniors. I had grown well attached to Ralph and

Mrs. J. in so short a time, though as someone said 'The country grows 'em that way'. Maybe so, but I still saw them as *specially* special people, though I doubted they would see it that way.

After church I went as planned to meet Richard and see something of Juneau. All was well now with his boss who was delighted to have tracked down his whereabouts and found him safe. Across the frozen lake the Mendenhall Glacier rose high above us, a massive fortress of blue ice that swept back into vast snowfields. Resplendent in its towering heights it dwarfed everything. It was a strange sensation to be standing below such a soaring edifice; cliff giants that reduced us to the smallest speck in the grand order of things. A feeling that grew as we stood and became even smaller, perhaps to invisibility. Yet we had a place there. A sense of belonging persisted. Our part in the whole was as a drip of water in an ocean, an ice splinter in a blizzard or single grain of beach or desert sand. The insignificant made significant, in a magnetic link, a necessary connection to comprise the whole. Fortunately, Richard was sensitive to allowing space.

The evening glistened as we watched the lights on the harbour ice. Tiny craft were clasped to the shore in its grip. Further out, ice chunks flecked the harbour like sails. Juneau was not usually this iced up, though to me it was the first time the sun felt warm. Even so, it was still difficult to believe that this had once all been tropical, so long, long ago.

Back home Mrs. J. had been waiting for me. I saw why. Ray was with her. An upright, responsible Ray, wanting to apologise for the night before. Hal came in battling a stubborn lurch. Ray helped him upstairs, the way Ralph had supported Ray the night before. Mrs. J. was well content and showed it all over her face.

Specks of wonder in simple, straightforward humanity. People as they are at heart.

I could almost see myself settling here, but that wasn't the plan; so much more to see and do, despite the harsh tear of parting. It was a guest house, with many more guests to come – and to go, as Richard had to. Now, was my time to go.

Grace

The spirit of St. Vincent flowed from its people. Their energy permeated its streets, its shores and its churches. You could feel it washing over you in a wave that cried out for expression. To be understood, but open to understanding. To give or receive.

The colourful Caribbean island was other things too, some of them bloody; a surprise at first amid so much openness, but drugs dealt in person or gangs, transform humanity. At the other extreme was the family shop on the hillside that sold unboxed chicken eggs from their own strutting hens and ladled out home-made Mauby, which they made from the bark of the Mauby tree growing in their backyard; a drink not unlike sarsaparilla. Produce was weighed on old type market scales with brass scoop on one side and iron weights of varying measure in lbs. and ozs. on the other. I almost expected to be charged in £'s. s. d - old style LSD.

Storms, were spectacular. With the aid of a Minister at 'ground level' I was welcomed into a lively community house three-quarters of the way up one of the islands many mountains. With views at each twist and bend, reaching ever outward, shelter could not have been more beautifully placed.

But then came …the torrent of rain that beat the ground was so fierce that the ground became warm. Thunder boomed close; soon I was standing ankle deep on the tiled floor of the open-sided terrace hall. Though Sunday, clearly the elements were not having a day of rest. Then, the force of a lightning and thunder strike in unison directly and low overhead blasted apart the adjacent mountain. Instinctively I ducked, hands over ears, and dropped to the floor. When it seemed safe to look up, I couldn't believe what I saw. Surely the mountain couldn't still be there after that ear bludgeoning explosion, so close? But it was. And seemingly still in one piece. I started, then stopped laughing at myself when I realised that every dog, of which there were many, was barking and charging about wildly. Almost as extreme as my own reaction. Why? Surely they were used to it!

'But they are not' I was told, when skies had cleared and I was further down the hill en route to the town. People had come out of their houses to exchange wonderment at the storm. The rain had stopped, but water continued to cascade down streets and hillside. Each spoke of their amazement at the storm. I was surprised that me and the dogs weren't alone in our response. The people express without restraint, the beautiful, wondrous, frightening, and the unexpected. And like the people themselves, every storm is different.

Down in a watery, muddy town, splashing beneath the sunshine, I was told the service of the church I was about to enter lasted for three hours. I recalled the all-night services in Swaziland. I had grave doubts that I could stay awake for a whole night but went anyway. Every moment was alive and sleep was nowhere near. The night was energetic, spontaneous joy and wonder that flew by, so what was three hours? I entered.

When the service finished, I doubted it had lasted an hour let alone three. My watch must be wrong, only it wasn't. The service *had* lasted three hours, plus.

The familiar much-loved songs, not heard for so long, the sermon, the people around me, all touched me deeply. My body and emotions were suddenly not my own, or perhaps very much my own considering the depths from which they were being raised. Their escape was building within me, I continued singing. I'd been this close once before; a volcano due to erupt, but suppressed by controlling circumstances. Time and place were not in tune, and health paid the toll, as it always had. This time was different. Here, no destructive self-discipline necessary. No fear of consequences. Here only understanding and love.

The service was coming to a close. At its end, I stood and looked for a face I could approach. It didn't take long. Without fear or shame, I asked 'Is there someone I can cry with?' No hesitation or question. The lady went straight to someone, brought us together, and left. The two of us went to a pew where Grace hugged and held me to her comforting form. Tears more than half a century old broke through the dam to soak her, previously pristine, white blouse. Grace was not her name, though Grace she had in abundance. Gloria too suited her perfectly. But I'll call her Grace. Grace prayed with me and asked that I might be helped through my loss. No words had been exchanged regarding my overflow. Grace spoke as she felt but I strongly denied bereavement and she continued to re-assure in general terms. Understanding without knowing. Understanding without questioning.

Bereavement to me was the loss of a close and dear friend, relative, or loved one. I had a week to think about it, after which time, I had to see Grace and tell her she was right. She had understood what I had not. So many forms of loss. One can mourn the loss of something never had, never likely to have and never could have, painfully so if it's deliberately and unnecessarily withheld, then taken to the finality of the grave by the perpetrator. Grace knew me better than I knew myself.

The following week I didn't have to seek out Grace. *She* came to me. I told her of my revelation. She smiled knowingly and lovingly as if she had expected my words and was pleased.

When the Service was about to start we went back to our respective seats; I didn't see Grace again, not even at the end of the service. Not surprising perhaps as it was a large church and took at least four hymns of many verses to get everyone through Communion. The music held me. I started to leave but couldn't and came back. Once more I tried. Another door this time: with the same result. The organ songs were certainly compelling, but was that the entire reason? I had no idea. Then the music stopped. There was one more door open to me; one more direction to try. With nothing to stop me, I strode out. On the top step I hesitated. Then I heard my name being called.

I couldn't see anyone, and strangely didn't recognise the voice. After a few more calls still without recognising the voice, though I don't know why, I saw Grace coming towards me. 'Joan, there is a breakfast served next door in the hall if you'd like to come". I thanked her but said I wasn't hungry but asked if she was going? "No, I don't have time. I thought you might want to. I can show you" I agreed that a cup of tea might be good and we went together. At the moment when I thought we would be saying our farewells Grace changed her mind and came in with me. We sat together, drank tea and ate home-made banana bread. Yummy!

This was Grace's time. It came slowly, softly. I felt privileged that she wanted to share it with me. Her personal story is not necessary to record. Enough to say that she survived, and was still surviving the aftermath. No tears fell from *her* eyes. Maybe they were still to come or maybe she had already cried herself dry. She spoke as before, gently, without bitterness or malice. She was stating life with all the depth of feeling and hurt it could give, but with the simplest and purest of detachment. Not the detachment of one hard and insensitive, but as one who has succeeded in burying her theft of happiness in honest forgiveness: a great achievement that takes guts, self-assurance, and preparedness to stand alone. A wise woman with great understanding, radiating strength and softness in her tall and elegantly clothed bearing. She renewed in me the many meanings of loss as well as the many meanings of love. She had them all. I only knew about them. She *was* them. A wonderful woman in so many ways.

And what of the one who brought us together? Had she acted with knowledge or intuition, or was her choice spontaneous, in the moment?

Communication is a plexus of meandering paths – with its own maps.

Celebrations - Decorated and Undecorated

Swaziland, a tiny, beautiful Kingdom ruled by King Mswati III consists of three sections; high, middle and low veldts. Mbabane the capital was in the high veldt, and the King was about to have a birthday. I had missed the ceremony of the reed dance when maidens bring and dance with fresh reed gifts for the Queen Mother's new kraal fencing. But a Chief's wife I sometimes visited gave me the surprising news that anyone can go to the King's birthday, which he celebrates for three days.

The sit-down meal and tiered cake on 14th Sept., for his 33rd birthday was by invitation only, but the following two days were open to anyone. I was four or five days late in hearing the news of the American tragedy on 11th Sept., but the King apparently stopped his private birthday meal to pray and express grief at such sad news in the midst of rejoicing… and took the opportunity to ask the guests not to steal the cutlery!

On the third and last day, I arrived. Fields inclining upward were spread with stalls, people cooking and selling food, drinks and anything you could possibly want – and not want. Towards the top of more fields, sounds changed. Celebrations came into view, spread on the flat head of the hill.

Outside the main enclosure, a multitude of

dancers in traditional dress bare-breasted on one side only were warming up bodies and voices before parading and chanting inside for the King and his family. The ground vibrated with the pounding of their feet. Fine, strong young women, with great energy and smiles, they welcomed me to join them. Before they entered the arena, I was pleased to dance with them, following their steps. Swazi TV was also active and my views were part of the recorded mix apart from the dancing.

Inside the enclosure, I expected to sit on the grass with hundreds of other spectators. Surprisingly I was shown to a chair under a marquee, where I sat behind a row of warriors clad in loincloths, feathers, and armbands of woven hair. To my left, the Royal marquee. The King in ceremonial dress sat with two of his seven wives and the Queen Mother whose title literarily means She Elephant. Doesn't sound flattering? But here, it is as complimentary as is the King's title of Lion. After all, any animal becomes as welcome or otherwise according to the attributes we give it and associate it with. For instance, in the west the owl is a symbol of wisdom. In India it symbolises stupidity and in Africa, evil. So if referred to as an owl, its meaning would hinge entirely upon where you were at the time.

The maidens, dancing and singing came endlessly and kept coming. There were said to be thousands of them. Not too hard to believe.

Carrying shields and short-bladed weapons they paraded closer in front of the Royal Family.

This is the time when the King traditionally chooses another wife. This year he would not. It was his example of highlighting AIDS awareness. Was this perhaps the reason the King wore only two love letters round his neck? A King would surely have more.

'Yes' said a self-appointed translator, also under the marquee 'the King has many love-letters. So many, he wears them two at a time'

Zulu love-letters are written in coloured beadwork. A romantic way of expressing love before writing was the norm:

White (bone) *Purity, cleanliness, true love.*

Black (shadow) *Anger, hurt (my heart has become as black as the hut rafters, as I hear you have taken another maiden)*

Red (blood) *Intense love. (My heart bleeds for you)*

Blue (dove) *Faithfulness and calm (if I was a dove I would fly the endless skies to you)*

Green (grass)	*Love-sickness and jealousy (I've become as thin as a blade of grass from pining for you)*
Yellow (corn)	*Wealth or lack of it*
Pink (poverty)	*She doubts he will be able to afford her 'lobola'* [3]
Brown (earth)	*My love is like the earth. It gives rise to new life.*

Then came the warriors. To my surprise, in solo they danced in the same skilled, energetic, yet graceful balance and form, as did the Iban Chiefs of Borneo. More, they offered snuff, tobacco, beer and meat to the spirit of a departed male, also the custom in Borneo. One outstandingly energetic warrior clad in light coloured skins was said to have been King Zwelithini, the Zulu King of South Africa, Kwazulunatal, who has his own Reed ceremonies, but …

Dancing went on till King Mswati, a head above his warrior entourage, went down to the maidens, moving along their ranks and bowing his thanks to them. The King's gold-headed sceptre (usually black) shone even more brightly in the sun, way

---

[3] Bride price in cattle

above the triangular headed sceptres of his entourage.

Following the King's example of AIDS awareness, the Chief of the maidens, denoted by the black feathers in her hair, announced the return, two weeks back, of Umcwasha, a blue and yellow skein hanging from the back of the head that says the wearer is abstaining from sex for five years. For those who had had sex but wished to wear Umcwasha, a black and red skein could be worn, the same colours as for older girls not in a relationship, but wishing to be left alone. What puzzled me was that there was no starting age. It seemed to be from whatever age one chose or was at when the scheme came into force.

The King himself warned all men not to touch any Umcwasha maiden. Apart from no sex, this also meant no handshaking, but set greetings were to be observed on meeting. Boy and girl together were to be chaperoned wherever possible. If a boy touches, or in any way violates the rule, his family will be fined one cow. The same for a girl violating the rule by wearing trousers with Umcwasha. If the girl becomes pregnant, both parties will be fined a cow. If no cow, then the equivalent in Emalangeni, cash, must be paid. Those breaking the edict will be tried by chiefs, whose judgment cannot be challenged in any court. Parents were expected to encourage their children to observe the rules.

A new life by recognising past traditions as

relevant today. May there still be time. My willing interpreter had been invaluable.

The festivities were finished now and people wandered off to the area of the King's residence, a pleasant pink bungalow, here in Nlangano, and naturally not his main residence. A pile of long reeds leaned into each other like a tall slender tepee. Brought by the maidens, not for the Queen Mother this time but for the King, they were to reinforce his kraal fence. Here, for his own fun the King danced and chanted. For as long as he did so, so would his warriors, who seemed to enjoy the informality. Even close up the King was a good head taller, and not because any of the 60 or so warriors were short. There was a food marquee, surprisingly for everyone, to which I was invited. We ate and drank and the King was still dancing. The food supplied and consumed was endless.

The word 'maiden' today has a wider meaning. At one time the chosen ones were expected to be virgins. Now 'maiden' can include any girl who has not had a baby or been pregnant. Another reason perhaps, why not to add to the King's wives. She may not be a virgin, and as such could be a risk to the Royal family. Virginity was no longer left to the judgment of the non-drooping or unbroken reed[4].

When the great day was finished, people moved en masse through the fields. Truckloads of maidens,

---

[4] It used to be said that if a girl is not a virgin her reed will droop or break

equipment, pots, pans and all kinds of utensils and tables were on the move. Every kind of vehicle was full to overflowing. By the time I reached a seething road, the last bus had gone, leaving just as many people heaving about as before. I started walking. A cabby stopped and said he could catch up with the bus to Mbabane. I told him I only had the bus fare but he assured me it wouldn't be far, because it hadn't long gone. It was a long deserted walk, lifts seemed rare, darkness was coming, and I wasn't comfortable about sleeping out. I was persuaded and still bathing in the glow of a great day, I got in.

After a bit, when no bus appeared, I wanted out. The short distance wasn't even worth the bus fare but angrily he stopped. I got out. So did he. I must have more money. When he realised I'd told him the truth and that's why I was leaving, his rantings and arm waving, grew even more wild and loud. I was at a loss. I couldn't stay here. Neither could I stay with him. Why didn't he go so that I could think about what best to do?

There had been no one on the road, till... I was only aware of her presence with her last few determined steps, into the face of the driver. There was no doubt she was telling him what she thought of him in his own language. Then, in English:

'I know you. I've seen you singing in the choir on Sundays, then week-days you behave like this?' His anger juddered defensively down to a low resentful muttering. Finally, he got back in and drove off in a dusty indignant huff, leaving the two of us. We exchanged party stories at the side of the road. Thalia as I shall call her, had been to a Lobola[5] party, and had left later than intended. To me, her timing was perfect. An Angel of the Night for which I was truly thankful. My idea was to walk on up to an isolated petrol station. In the light you can see the driver plus any rapport with the attendant can help. Also, there may just be a toilet.

To my surprise, Thalia said 'No. Better stick to the road', even though she too now had a need. We passed the garage and walked further. When matters became urgent, on an earth banked roundabout, Thalia openly squatted. Since we were in this together, I was pleased to follow her lead. Besides, natural functions here were more readily accepted, though I still felt decidedly conspicuous, picked up in every passing headlight.

Thalia's strength of character and confidence balanced a good warm heart, with the knowledge of how to use it. She could have been emotionally vulnerable but I felt she had a strategy with a good foundation. Hitching at night was not my choice but with Thalia it was quite different. Thalia got the lifts and sat in front to do the talking, while I sat in the back.

From previous experience, I knew it was better to be someone's personal friend. Someone whose

---

[5] Money or goods to be paid to a family to marry their daughter. Party for agreement

roof one has slept under and received hospitality from. When asked about me Thalia did just that, 'Oh a long time. We're old friends'. My stomach leapfrogged as I realised I knew nothing about her or her family, other than the name of her village. But I needn't have worried. Her response was accepted without question; every time. She was well respected and held in high esteem by all she met.

Another lift asked if we wanted to go somewhere and have some fun, but it was only a suggestion and not mentioned again after Thalia said she needed to get home. On our last lift her response to going on somewhere was, 'Another time' and left him with a sisterly kiss on the cheek and a phone number. Everyone was happy. In this way we finally reached Mbabane, where we parted.

From having a good day celebrating, to facing the alternatives after missing the last bus, my spirits had taken a dive. Never did I expect a selfless guiding light to appear at that exact lowered point to lift me up again. Thalia didn't have to extend her night travel skills to include me, but she did. What a woman! Thank you.

A down to earth birthday - undecorated:

It was Christmas. A much played down
Christmas. Some said this was because of Malawi's
Muslim President and Christmas coincided with Id-
el-Fitr. Others said it was the economy that made it
too expensive and increased crime. For the same
reason there were no midnight services: an open
invitation to have the house raided.

People were glad when President Bhanda died.
They would have freedom of speech. He was a
harsh dictator. Now they talked of him fondly.
Under him, everyone had work, money, food, land,
at least one goat and a roof. Now there was less of
everything except crime.

Towns were quiet with no signs of decoration or
celebration.

Villages seemed freer and in an open, sandy
area, I followed the sound of singing. It led me to a
hall. Of itself, the bare, grey stone walls and floor
looked bleakly formidable. But this illusion was
totally swept away by Sisters from a nearby school
who were making their own all singing, all dancing
Christmas party. They welcomed me in through
their one source of light – the open door. No
windows. What a tribute to their enthusiasm,
determination and spirit, though I doubted they
saw it that way. They were here to enjoy
themselves and celebrate in whatever space there
was, spreading the fun to anyone around, while

doing so.

There are few gatherings where excited energy and laughter could be enjoyed so abundantly in such sparse conditions. No decorations, no food, no drink of any kind, not even a chair. The people themselves furnished the hall. If anyone wanted to stop dancing, the concrete floor was space enough to sit, but no-one did. Voices made the music to which we continually danced in a circle.

Sometimes one of the dancers would give us steps to follow, going faster and faster till we could no longer keep up and collapsed in breathless laughter. Other times we danced till someone suddenly signalled us to stop. No one should move. To much laughter, I was usually the one to stop late but most excitement and clapping came when I got it right. Laughter was becoming an intoxicant.

I don't know how long we danced but I enjoyed every moment and when I left, uplifted and refreshed, the glow of the party came with me. A party that lacked nothing because every vital and genuine ingredient came entirely from themselves; that amazing commodity - people. All the decorations, comforts and conveniences could not have added one jot more good, nourishing energy. It was there in abundance with enough to wrap ourselves in and take away in a warm glow.

We had definitely celebrated Christmas.

Man Out of Place

Fifteen slow hours and the train finally pulled in to Lusaka. It was late afternoon and my goal, Cairo Road, was way out across a different railway line.

Beyond the dusty grass and dry bald spaces, two razed blocks of debris; now permanent rubbish tips, lay desolate. An approaching electrical storm spread an ethereal light. Birds squawked their demands at each other, dogs fought for the best pickings. The only human life amongst the rubble, was solitary, distant figures. They moved as if through mud; unaware of their surroundings. I wandered on towards the track so overgrown it was hardly visible. No train had seen these rails for aeons. Beyond: more devastation. How far did this ghost land extend?

Across the line, a figure scrabbled about in the rubble. Further down the track on this side, someone with a strange rolling gait slowly came to a halt. He fumbled with his belt, then slowly took down his trousers, and began examining his genitals. He was no threat. I doubted he was even aware of my presence. Inside his own world, he was just doing what had to be done in the moment.

Lightning broke up the sky. The fireworks of an

electric storm had begun. Pink and blue flares fanned flashing from behind tiered cloud banks. A spectacle without rain, or sound of any kind. Storms like this magnetised me. Cairo Road could wait. I turned to leave as one drawn in hypnotic trance. It was then that I noticed him. And came back to earth.

A tall, lone figure: different. Different in the way he stood; upright, regal but not stiff, relaxed. A man connected to his surroundings. Curious I walked passed him at a distance. As I drew level he looked at me openly. Then, with a slight bow, he said 'Good Evening'. His politeness was in no way subservient. I stopped. We talked.

I can't remember a single word or phrase of anything we said. I can only remember the man himself. The condition of his clothes totally belied the person he radiated. Neither his apparel nor his setting could hold him. He shone through them both as if they did not exist. A man out of place I thought – but no. This man would be 'in place' wherever he found himself. His attitude and manner would still have been appropriate had he been standing in marble halls. Unlike the others I'd seen, he was alive in himself, despite that his once white collar, perfectly in place above faded shirt, was now brown with constant wear, and his carefully knotted tie was shiny and colourless with grease. A long overcoat reached down over trousers to shoes so cracked they could never look polished.

Footwear that gave little protection but was a symbol of a one time value that now held a different worth, perhaps even more important - his memories. He had clothed himself in his memories and wore them with pride like armour that melded perfectly, held him up, and could never tarnish. He *was* his memories, his own past life.

Gracious, aristocratic and softly spoken, he asked for nothing. Wanted nothing. It was me who wanted something. I wanted to ask how he slept, found food, kept dry, but felt it would offend. He was his own person, totally self-sufficient, yet how? There was no sad story, no bitterness, no blame or resentment. He exuded a sensitive, noble gentleness. A man always 'at home' with himself. No matter where, he would always be himself. It was where he lived, inside someone he was always true to. What was his secret I wondered. It was something to think about, and I did.

The light was changing again. I moved on as sounds began to wake. I looked back and watched him merge with the new light, standing tall and still, a pillar on a barren horizon. I felt I had known this man intimately, the truth is, I most probably didn't know him at all. Perhaps it was enough that he knew himself so well and I would just have to be content with that. Or perhaps his secret was that he knew without doubt the value of memories, our own individual history.

47

The rain began to fall. A fork of lightning cracked through the sky. Drips turned to blobs and built to a thunderous speed and force as I reached the edge of the ghost land. The rain closed the scene, like a final curtain falling on a privileged spotlight of hidden life.

Good Tidings

Boxes, bundles and bodies moved in conglomerate mass to wait at the Mozambique border. Buses would not be crossing from there into Malawi. The sponge-like press fell apart and spread out on the ground, changing, moving, getting itself comfortable. No orderly queue, but a picnic, as eating, drinking, partying and impromptu joyful and rousing services erupted. And why not? It was said that to get safely through Mozambique, one must pray twice.

I was here to see the June 2001 solar eclipse as well as see southern Africa. But to be on the line of totality, I had to find a suitable place that was also accessible. There was still time and it wasn't my choice to be leaving Malawi. Emotionally, I was still there: the people had wound themselves into my heart. I was leaving to satisfy a more than patient Immigration. My visa, despite its many extensions had long expired.

I wrapped myself for one last time, into the warmth of the people.

With no idea I was behaving strangely, I had been 'hijacked' to a local hospital. Why? For what reason? Stay in? What for? Severe Malaria? Certainly not. I didn't shake, quake or ache. 'You have a choice' said the medical officer. Good I thought. We can go home. No I couldn't. My choice was 'Room or ward?' I was staying.

Malawi had so little. No doctors or nurses. Clinical Officers treated, and were good at their individual skill, be it tending wounds or delivering babies. My C.O. was a cheerful Vincent, specialising in Malaria. With no bedpans, gowns, food, water, linen, I smiled when told I would have a guardian, assuming they meant, as was often the case, ancestor protection or guardian angel; not so. *Everyone* had to have a guardian: to bring food, clean drinking water, to wash what's needed including the patient, looing at the pit toilet outside and to hold the stick to pull up on, from a weakened squat position. I smiled again as I thought of my appointed guardian. It was 'hi-jacker' Angela from the CCAP[6] hostel where I was staying: about as close to an angel as anyone could get, and not only by name. Angela did things for me that my own mother wouldn't have done.

Drifting in and out of consciousness someone was always there beside my bed. I was never alone. Words of encouragement and uplifting prayer from people I knew and strangers I came to know, like two young people Dennis and Lyten and assistant chaplain Elizabeth who gave me a memorable cold water wash.

Nights were noisy with comforting family

---

[6] Central Church of Africa Presbyterian

closeness. The ward was full. Patients filled the beds. Guardians, filled the blanketed floor, with themselves, their children and those of their patients, and with baskets of food. Fans whirred, babies cried, adults moaned, sobbed and occasionally screamed. Angela had no need to stay. Food was wasted on me, even water could do an about-turn.

Humour, smiles, including from Vincent, willed everyone lovingly to get better. Here was something the west had lost: the art of healing as well as treating. No-one was alone or in need. Lack of facilities was more than made up for in care and good-will. The only exception was the Chaplain who blew in accusing, 'You must not blame God. These things happen. You must make your peace with God. Make your peace, now'. It hadn't occurred to me to blame God. Or was he telling me I was dying? Puzzled, I told him I didn't blame God, which rather took the wind from his sails. In fact I had a lot to be thankful for. The high-strength antibiotics to clear a stubborn poisoned leg had been thorough. They had killed the good as well as the bad bacteria and disguised the symptoms of malaria, except to Angela, who had acted swiftly. That's a lot to be thankful for. 'Well, when you walked into one wall, bounced off, hit the other and lurched on ....'

It was also Angela who said that one night in hospital I was fighting to breathe. Sounded like me, though I had no memory of it. But I did remember calmly watching and feeling my strength drain away, and casually thinking, 'So this is what it's like to die. Just slowly disappearing. Quite peaceful really'.

Then with a sudden jolt, something penetrated and I hung on to what was left of my core, now at my feet, as Dennis or Lyten's voice came to me. They had been reading the 23rd Psalm and it was the words 'He restoreth my soul… that had reached me. What was I doing? I stopped 'letting go' and mentally repeated the words till I'd reversed 'letting go', and was tugging fervently on the last bit of shadow, drawing it up till I'd wrapped myself back into life. Two people? two worlds? A wondrous delirium? Whatever it was, I was back. I could feel myself whole again.

Around my third I.V of quinine, the two ladies opposite, reading their Bibles as they often did, were sitting up in bed, backs erect, well groomed and elegant in silky blouses tied at the neck. Such striking figures only revealed themselves now that they were dressed to go home. They finished their scriptures, closed their Bibles, carefully set them aside, then in unison, left their beds and slowly came to mine.

Kneeling, they began to pray. Their voices rose gradually, becoming louder and stronger; their bodies and limbs joined the sound, moving, writhing, energy racking their being. In full sway there came a dramatic transformation. Their entire countenance changed. Lids snapped open, two huge round orbs stood out, rolling. Seeing yet not seeing. Their eyes in different faces were 'gone'. Were they speaking Chechiwa? Chitumbuka? the two languages spoken on the ward apart from English. Or Sangoma[7], words that meant something only to a Sangoma?

Shakily their hands touched everything around me; chanting over each thing in turn in the only words I recognised 'There is no disease in this....' whatever it happened to be. The shaking grew violent and I was afraid it would dislodge the needle in my vein or block the IV, but they cleansed that as well. Then their hands felt gently but directly on my body with the chant 'There is no disease in this body, there is no disease...'. A comic touch, when they found my briefs drying on a rail under the bed, and swung them around their heads rubbing their manicured hands over them in the air, repeating 'There is no disease in this garment'.

No-one attempted to interrupt their flow but I felt some agitation filtering through the ward. Certainly not from me. I felt something good in what they were doing. Not that anything *could* penetrate such fervour but when I smilingly thanked them, the convulsions and chanting began to abate. Slowly a calm passed over the passion,

---

[7] Medicine woman, shaman or female witch-doctor

and they became once again their serene, poised, elegant selves.

One of the two women offered to take me to the 'loo', a chance not to be missed. While I squatted, my benefactor urged 'You must leave here. Get out or you will die. There are people here who want to kill you'. I felt no such thing from anyone, not even from the person in front of me, warning me. I thanked her but said I couldn't go anywhere right now, too weak. As I hauled myself up the stick she held for me, the sangoma entreated 'Remember, they want you dead', but still I could not fear, even in that vulnerable position. There was only love and trust.

When we returned, her friend was shaking and chanting over my vacated bed, cleansing it of all disease. As we drew near she stopped and both helped me back into bed. I felt only good will from them. Goodbyes were exchanged as if all had been routine, which to them it was. A concerned Elizabeth apologised but I felt privileged that they had wanted to do it, and I *didn't* mention the conversation in the loo. That was a mystery to think on. Though already I had something of an answer. Thinking was different in Africa.

With the last of the quinine, Angela surprised me by saying we were going home.

Back at the hostel caring continued till I could recognise myself in the mirror. Even the two wads of fat that had camped on my hips since I was about 12 years old, weren't there. Who *was* that person? We'd never met before. A rare chance to see my face as one would see a stranger. What could I read in it? Did I even like that person?

The British High Commission rang to see if I wanted to be flown back to the UK. I thanked them but said I couldn't be better looked after than where I was, which was true. The Hostel had been keeping them informed.

Only lemons tasted as they should. With lemon juice, water stayed down. Tea too had to be saturated with lemon juice. I craved and devoured lemons avidly. One day the seller of lemons visited without lemons. No lemons! There were none in the market. Poor woman scuttled off with her basket. She returned - with limes. Better than nothing, but... what was it with me and lemons? I had become an addict.

My sight was blurry but hearing wasn't as bad as the reputation that Quinnine suggested. Angela picked and boiled peach, guava and avocado leaves as medicine, drunk of course with oodles of lemon juice. When they could be found, potato leaves gave iron.

Visitors included Dennis and Lyten and the understanding face of Immigration. Sympathetic to the situation they suggested periodic checkups with the hospital, receipts for which I must take to

Blantyre Immigration office, close to the Mozambique border. It was generous, an unofficial extension without a fine. How ever slowly, a return visit to Vincent might also answer a question that was bothering me.

To add to my weakness and still green urine Vincent told me I had acquired a heart murmur. 'But I am not expert in this field. When you are back, you must get it checked. (I did. Vincent was too modest. He was right, a mitral murmur).

I didn't need to ask the question that was bothering me. Vincent gave me the answer. 'You know they are still talking about you'. Hmmh. Here it comes I thought. I was afraid they would be upset that I had not paid for a private room (which gave no more than privacy) which would help to support the hospital. Vincent went on quoting, 'Oh that Joannah[8], she doesn't care. No private room like European lady. She comes in with *us* '. That was *not* what I had expected, but what a relief. They weren't at all upset that I had chosen to be in a ward. To me, being with them was to my benefit, they had nourished me and I was grateful. I hadn't expected that they would see it that way.

Weeks passed, during which time I was thrilled to stay up for the whole day. I progressed to walking along the wall to the end of the building. Then getting to the shower and actually having one.

---

[8] Joan was confused with John. Joannah was preferred

To regain balance and stamina tried simple yoga movements. Only it wasn't my body I was working with. I just wasn't inside it yet. Later, without my thighs - no feeling, only space where they ought to have been, I got to the post office but couldn't stand in line; made it to the market, to buy lemons of course amongst other fruit but couldn't carry it back. Disgruntled with my tardy progress, I was surprised when someone who said he was a colleague of Vincent, expressed surprise at seeing me, 'Oh Vincent will be so pleased when I tell him I've seen you out without a guardian'. I didn't know I was still supposed to have one, so maybe I wasn't doing so badly.

My eating went from one extreme to the other. Investigating a steaming cauldron at the side of the road, I had a trial run. From lemons to …cowheel! It was more jelly than meat but fatty. Fatty was not my kind of food, but it reminded me of my grandmother. It was delicious, and I noshed daily. Must have had something I needed because it stayed down. Not that I had given up on lemons. Oh no.

My final visit to Vincent, gave me vitamin tablets, and necessary paperwork. I still felt vulnerable at the thought of travelling. Yet a faint current tingled through me, at the thought of movement, newness. My send-off came with spectacular hail-stones the size of ping-pong balls and overhead storms that halted cooking for fear of lightning striking the exposed kitchen wires (a common sight).

The 5 a.m. bus left at 11 a.m.

Storms, break-downs, detours. The final mechanical fault could only be fixed at Lilongue bus station, a place I had purposely avoided when choosing a route because of its crime. I especially wanted a smooth running life right now; the only kind I could handle. But the one place with the right part and facilities for repair was where we didn't want to be. Passengers argued for a relief bus. There wasn't one. Staying the night was no one's choice.

When we arrived, the bus station had a silent, eerie feel about it. I went to the supervisor's office. She phoned H.O. who confirmed still no relief bus. She gave me a chair which confirmed a lengthy wait. 'It could have been worse. You could have come this morning. One side of the yard was covered in blood and bits' she said waving her arm over the concourse. 'It's only just got cleared.' This was not comforting news though she probably meant it to be. A driver had asked a passenger he saw pick-pocketing another passenger what he was doing. In response, the pickpocket stabbed the driver with a screwdriver. Blood spurted and the man collapsed. Despite the blood loss he was alive when taken to hospital and hopefully he survived his courageous act. No chance for the perpetrator though. The crowd tore him to pieces: mob justice. 'When police arrive at a scene like that it's usually to protect the wrongdoer' she explained. For that one it was too late. The blood and bits she spoke of belonged to the thief. Presumably dogs cleared what was left.

The relief bus (relief in more ways than one), when it eventually came, many hours later, took us passed jelly mould mountains, plateaus and gorges, to arrive in Blantyre in darkness.

There were various possibilities out of Blantyre, even a cargo/refugee plane but Immigration gave me a reprieve by asking for a ticket out from the border on a bus that not only was said to be going but had a good chance of actually going, which was probably why the cheapest bus ticket would not suffice. Second cheapest was passable with a ticket dated a few days ahead. This gave time to see Malawi's highest mountain Mulanje and surrounding vast tea growing area.

It was a wet journey over unmade roads, potholes and backs of waterlogged pickups, surrounded by the usual cheery company. A tall dark fir-tree forest broke the ocean of tea plantations. The last part was a refreshing walk in bright moonlight. Mist swirled up the folds of pink-tinged mountains. Clouds and a rainbow graced Mulanje's many peaks. Below her, sorghum, millet, cedars and acacias; all cloaked in silence except for the birds.

At the end of the slow haul up to the camping ground, I sank luxuriously and unexpectedly into a flat at hostel prices. Comfort and beauty in the mountains. Would I ever leave? I slept to the sound of trickling streams.

At 3 a.m. I got up and went outside. The sky had cleared. Stars hung big and brilliant. A lather of Milky Way and a clear southern cross. The moon filtered its light through the tall pines. Enchantment.

Mulanje heralded morning, wearing a cloud necklace. The force of falling water hitting a boulder-strewn galloping stream resounded. Rich green and brazenly colourful plants; all played their part in the magical mystery of dawn. Out of sight voices, echoed through wooded hills around the mountains in ethereal harmony.

No wonder I felt so at home. Not just from nature's peace and beauty, but here too I discovered was under the auspices of the CCAP. Perfect, peaceful, timing.

Leaving such a tonic was a big effort. My body still wasn't quite mine and my urine was still green: was there ever any other colour? Nevertheless, I was on top of the world. Even my need for lemons was no longer desperate.

* * *

The bus to the border wasn't coming. Joining the resultant clamouring mass we shrank ourselves and bundles tightly into a combie and disgorged ourselves into the good-humoured picnic and song we were now enjoying, to await departure. I was in no rush to leave. Which was just as well. Both buses arrived but neither was going anywhere. With bodies well rusted, the engines were good and drivers of anything on wheels were, of necessity, good mechanics. The only difference I could see was that the cheaper bus had no passenger windows. Nothing serious. Also, I was mentally placing the last piece of puzzle to the warning given me in hospital by the Sangoma in the privacy of the toilet. Puzzle in that the words spoken were totally alien to what she was clearly radiating.

Since I could only feel love and trust from her, her warnings of death, I concluded, were designed to kick my own healing powers into urgent action. Showing how much life meant by challenging it, putting mine in danger in front of me to show its true value. A psychological nudge to spur me back to health.

A tremor of expectancy now permeated the air. So much day had passed. What was happening? No-one knew, but suddenly, excitedly we were climbing aboard – where we waited some more. Next to me sat a fit looking, ready-for-anything Samson of a man. He turned and introduced himself, 'Samson' he said extending a hand. Mmmmh! Ah well. His shrewd, searching eyes were placards forestalling trouble. He had no intention of being killed if he could shoot first. To that end he carried a handgun. With stories of bandits and gratuitous killings in Zimbabwe and South Africa, he was a companion to tip the odds. A student from Malawi introduced himself: 'Tidings, but you can call me Good' he smiled. I stuck with the name of 'Tidings'.

Eventually we were off and crossing the Tete Corridor, or 'gun-run' as it is called, from the transport of arms across it that fed the civil war: a war that left thousands of mines which still cause death and injury: and will do so for years to come, because that's how long they will take to clear. The town of Tete had been the headquarters of FRELIMO[9] who fought for independence from the Portuguese, which was finally attained in 1975.

* * *

A suspension bridge spanning the ubiquitous Zambezi, led on into Zimbabwe. The soggy 'road' had become even, sloppier. A notice proclaiming a detour to an 'improved route' looked promising and the bus slurped off. It was not long before the 'improved' road became worse than the one

---

[9] Front for the Liberation of Mozambique

relinquished. We lurched jerkily through the night over uneven mud.

Around 4 a.m. the bus stuck. Daylight showed how deeply the back wheels of the bus and front part of the luggage trailer had skewered into the mud. With no implements, it was digging and scooping with hands. Tidings, in gauzy white shirt attacked the mud vigorously. 'We must conserve our water and food' he whispered. Hours later a lone man driving a donkey cart offered his machete. Except for Samson, we were sitting ducks. Plenty of flat space to see anyone coming, only we wouldn't be going anywhere.

We were making no progress, not even with the aid of the machete and finally efforts were abandoned. Tidings was still as spotless as he'd been at the border. No mean feat. A skill I often admired in Africa. I recalled a bus driver who, at the end of a hot day, parked his bus at the desert's edge, built a fire on the mud floor of a shelter and by candlelight scrubbed and washed. Next morning, smart as an airline pilot stepping from a five-star hotel, he boarded his bus in impeccable uniform and cap taking with him the whitest fresh change of shirt on a hanger. What an accomplishment!

I wandered round to the front of the bus, and stopped. Our driver on the far side was staring back along the road, transfixed. Then he dropped to his knees in praise and Alleluyas. Was he seeing a vision? Others followed his gaze with the same result. Curious, I went to his side of the bus. Were we all hallucinating? The only signal that had gone through the ether was prayer. But there, coming towards us were three Afrikaaners driving a breakdown platform! But how and from where, remained a mystery. Chained and hooked up, the bus was free in minutes. A unique situation of chains bringing freedom! To tumultuous Alleluyas and clapping, the bus moved through its new found freedom, stopping only to return the donkey farmer's machete plus ten Rand in thanks.

We had passed the 'lesser' bus earlier. It was coping with manageable tyre problems. Now it caught up with us, and was soon laughing its socks off. With all its faults, it had two things we didn't. Wipers that worked, and lights. The valiant 'lesser', shared its light, in guidance through the blackness.

Eighteen hours later we were crossing nature's border, the Limpopo, into South Africa. Kipling's 'great, grey-green greasy Limpopo' at that moment presented a mono-black.

At Pretoria, Samson was home. We said our goodbyes, then I went in search of the bus to Swaziland. The driver rested with a 'cuppa'. I never expect ease or comfort when travelling, but neither do I court trouble, which was why I was here looking for a bus rather than from Jo'burg. My stomach more than my mind still held the memory of Malawi Bus Station. I continued looking for the

Swazi bus. There had to be one. Why couldn't I find it? The resting driver told me what I didn't want to hear. There was no bus from Pretoria, but my ticket was still valid with him on his bus to Jo'burg. Good of him under the circumstances and if Jo'burg it had to be, then travelling with familiar faces had its benefits.

* * *

When we drew into Jo'burg bus station with its armed patrol, it was dark. Tidings, who was still spotless white, was to be met by friends who weren't there yet. Meanwhile he carefully unwrapped what he had come to sell. Beautiful and delicate, carved wood and moulded clay figures that peopled village scenes busy with daily life. He hadn't been taught, it was simply something he enjoyed doing.

Then we looked for the Swaziland bus. And found it. It was leaving Monday. Today was Saturday. On the way back a lively spiritual gathering sprouted and we were invited. Gents to one half, ladies to the other. Not till a smiling someone plonked something on my head did I notice the women had their heads covered. Afterwards, we mingled with hugs and kisses and warm words said for our protection. It was then I realised I'd been enthusing joyously with a baby's nappy on my head – a clean one! Then in minutes, musical instruments, baskets, babies, belongings, all magically dissolved.

Not that a bus station is a choice place to stay but it felt safer with its armed patrol than anywhere outside. But by lunch-time next day, Tidings suggested we venture outside.

'It'll be alright, you'll be with me', he assured.

We had been outside about fifteen minutes when an old lady passed, then called back 'Hello Mumma Grey-hairs'. Pleased, I smiled back and returned her greeting. 'That's acceptance' said Tidings. Mumma grey-hairs was on a par with 'old and fat', meaning you're wise and prosperous. 'They don't often see a white face around here, unless they're being mugged' smiled Tidings. Perhaps because of his reassurance, I went with him where I would be wary of going in London. A short, wide underpass. I was about to say so when we were both on the floor.

My mind went into another realm as I was pulled back by an arm round my neck from behind and held backwards, while someone else felt over my front, then started ripping at my chitenga[10]. Being new, the material was slippery so it was tied extra tightly. The more he tugged, the more it tightened. They changed tactics. Lifted me up by it and shook. It remained tied but ripped around its length. Then came the fear that valuables were not

---

[10] A wrap-around length of material that was a gift from Malawi

all they wanted. They were going to give me the AIDS virus, for fun.

Suddenly everything stopped. I didn't dare move. What did it mean? Then Tidings was helping me up. The attackers had gone: on the instant. Why? Tidings had been more aware. There had been six of them. Four went to him and he had succeeded in keeping them from forcing his legs down. We started to walk out.

That's when I noticed. Across the mouth of the underpass stood a line of people four or five deep, silent, staring. What was Tidings reading I wondered. Most of them were women but I couldn't detect their purpose. We kept walking. At the last moment, they broke ranks to let us through. The only question one asked was 'Did they get anything?' We said we didn't know yet, but indicated my trailing torn chitenga. The women nodded slowly, seriously, with seeming restrained concern. We walked on unhindered.

It was a strange mugging. My watch and shoulder bag untouched and Tidings still wore his gold chain and cross. Had disapproving faces in the crowd stopped them? Had looks said 'we know who you are and you're in for a kicking for this attack?' They had their own laws.

Back in the bus station we sat, held hands and said the Lord's Prayer and 23rd Psalm. Anywhere else we would have been branded cranks; here it was as natural as breathing. People prayed anywhere, anytime. I felt bad that Tidings in protecting me had himself been mugged. Tidings felt bad that he had failed me. I recalled the protection we had been blessed with the night before. Some might sneer, but to have escaped being injured, robbed or raped in such a situation was indeed protection.

I brought coffee for us, then Tidings went off saying he needed something to cool his beating heart. He came back with two ice-creams which we took to the roof. Lovely, till we noticed the roof opened on to a main road on a higher level. We looked round cautiously. Not a mugger in sight! We stayed. Relaxed now, I laughed when Tidings said how good I was at screaming. 'Did you hear me screaming?' he asked. I hadn't. 'When I heard you, I thought, what a good idea, but you were better – started before you touched the floor'. I had no memory of screaming or any other reaction. Tidings prayed, and I must admit I felt no bad lingering aftermath of the mugging. Tidings had wiped the event clean. Clean was his speciality.

With the patrol alerted to events of the day, which Tidings thought might not be finished, we discussed sitting up all night in the tea tent. Its eye-watering fumes from the paraffin cooking stoves were too painful. Tidings suggested I sleep in the middle of other people outside by the fuel stand for protection. I squeezed myself into the line of bodies on the forecourt, a woman one side and a wife and husband on the other, but Tidings didn't join me. When I awoke a few hours later to change 'watch', he was adamant. He would not sleep but sat outside the tent.

Morning brought life back to the station. Tidings had indeed sat up all night. I left him at the tea tent, and went to pack up my bed. The husband of the woman I'd slept next to greeted me with two Rand (under 20 p.). It was mine, he said; found where I'd slept. I didn't think so. He was insistent. Later in the tea tent the woman who had slept on the other side of me, was fifty cents short of a 'cuppa', which I provided. Then, seated with our drinks, the wife came. She knelt beside me confidentially. 'My husband gifted you[11]. The money. It's mine'. It was now fifty cents short but Tidings was quick to make up the shortfall and I handed her the complete amount. She clenched her fists against taking the money, then stood up smiling and abruptly left. I was puzzled.

'What was that about?' asked Tidings. I explained. 'Go after her. It may not be finished'. I went back, insisted she must take what was rightfully hers; not happy with what isn't mine… Added clenched fists from other smiling sleepers pushed the rand back. Deadlock. My refusing the rand would deprive them of a blessing, they said and 'no', the blessing couldn't be shared. I must

---

[11] 'gave you a gift'

keep the money for their sake.

'Yes,' said Tidings, back in the tent, '- it was a test. You were a stranger in their fold. They wanted to know about you. A white face there is not usual'.

I wondered what would have happened if I hadn't passed the test, which I apparently had. He was grimly unforthcoming. After a pause, 'Then it would not be finished'.

Today the bus would go to Swaziland. Tidings said he would breathe easy only when I was safely on it. 'Strange things have been happening. I hope when you reach Swaziland they will stop'. I hoped so too, till he added 'But I think strange things will always happen to you'.

When the bus came, I was concerned that Tidings friends still had not arrived. He indicated a block of flats just outside the station. 'That's where they live.' I couldn't believe what he was saying. He could have gone to them any time, but chose not to. I looked at him dumbly. 'I couldn't leave you alone in such a place' he explained.

Malawans don't speak of honour, they have it.

Older Malawans had said that the young who steal today had far more than they had ever had, but turning to crime – never, for them unthinkable. They shook their heads in shame, sorrow and puzzlement. Tidings was twenty-five.

Now I understood his eternal whiteness. It was his armour shining through that prevented anything less, even after rolling on the floor during a mugging!

Two days in any bus station, hardly sounds desirable, yet crammed into it had been a life-pattern of warmth and learning.

When the bus left it was with relief that Tidings would also be leaving into safe hands.

Living the Highlife

On a bus going south towards Jordan's Rose Red City of Petra, I was having difficulty paying my fare to Karaak. The conductor was reluctant to take it; not as a kindly gesture but rather as if there was something wrong with it. But why? He was clearly uneasy.

Little by little it emerged that I was not going where I thought I was going. No, not Karaak. A Greek Orthodox priest had paid my fare to his desert parish of Ra'beh. There was no space for discussion, it was settled. Not that I wanted to change anything as the byways and sidetracks are often the zesty extras that add to a trip. There was time and I accepted his 'unorthodox' invitation.

Much later, through flat sandy landscape, priest 'Abonna' beckoned from the front of the bus. We had arrived.

Just the two of us got off and when the bus was out of sight there was only sandy brown to the horizon. Ra'beh was a small, brown, community that blended with the dryness of the sandy brown landscape. But it was by no means dead. As we got nearer, it erupted with sounds of excited laughter, shouts, and running feet over stony ground. We approached the noisy and enthusiastic welcome, which surprisingly came from a 'crowd' of just Mrs. Abonna, a friend and six girls. Their joyous excitement about everything simply exploded from them. When we came together, it was clear that Abonna was much loved by everyone: a man who held the community together with his own brand of 'unorthodox' humour. Then, still all talking at once, the girls decided to give me a tour of their community. I must start with the school. Their interest in absolutely everything was insatiable.

The one class school, housed 25 children who clapped, recited and sang lustily. Some stood on the benches to try and out-voice the others for exuberance. One boy recited so vociferously he slipped off the bench. Our smiles he could bear but not the giggles of the little girl beside him whom he was no doubt trying to impress. We clapped and banged our feet in time to the voices which went on and on till the older girls decided it was time to go somewhere else. We said our goodbyes and next stop was to a bare room, save for a small bath and dressing table.

Shoes off, mats were brought and we sat cross-legged. Being very 'proper', Abonna solemnly built a separating wall of mats between us to talk through. Then feigning deafness, one by one he took down a mat. This went on till he was looking 'aghast' at the demolished wall, and the 'realisation' that there was nothing separating us.

Abonna had taught them all three words of English, 'Highlife, Abonna, Leb'non'. One day he would take them all, and he wanted them to keep it in mind. With a mischievous twinkle he stroked his beard, while Mrs. Abonna indicated that she too had ideas as to what she would do in Leb'non, and what better time than now to start preparing? So what had I got that they could put on their faces? Everyone was going to be beautiful – right now. I disappointed them by only having a lipstick. But their excitement soon returned as they tried it on themselves and on each other.

'Highlife, Leb'non', said Mrs. Abonna wielding the lipstick. The little mirror was working overtime. Then Abonna who had left us for a moment, returned to offer mock disapproval at such frivolity. Then *he* spent more time in front of the mirror than anyone else, carefully combing his long hair into a bun and dressing his beard, all of which brought upon himself an abundance of teasing.

The girls had been planning something. Whatever it was, it was almost ready. We were *all* going to be beautiful, so now it was my turn. What was it to be I wondered that needed such preparation? In fact it was something I had already experienced twice that day.

For the third time I was going to have my feet washed. When passing lone sandy dwellings earlier, I was welcomed in to a foot washing. It was a practical gesture of hospitality for dry dusty feet. Nothing subservient, and very refreshing.

Now, seating me on a sheepskin the girls prepared water, soap and towels. When the washing began, Abonna covered his eyes with his hands and left the room, to return again almost immediately to offer his help. Splashed away, he retreated, but under Mrs. Abonna's laughing eyes, when the girls progressed up my legs – we were having far too much fun to stop at my feet – he returned and was attacked generously, with soapy water for his pains. It was by far the most entertaining foot bath of the day.

So much fun, energy and laughter had produced an appetite and sad to say my visit was responsible for the deaths of six pigeons. Not that I heard or saw them shot or cooked, but they arrived in that condition. We sat cross-legged on the mats and ate the meat with flat red speckled bread. Towards the end of the meal, curiosity drove me to look more closely at the red speckles in the bread - leggy red ants. Like the pigeons, definitely dead and obviously edible. As to taste, they could just as easily have been dried red currents – nothing scary.

When we had finished eating, still with Leb'non in mind, they all came to the road with me to wait for a lift. When a truck came by belching black smoke, Abonna wouldn't look at it and waved it on. There would be something better. When what he considered a more worthy vehicle came along, he let it stop. While making a fumbling search between the folds of his robe for his purse, the girls were jumping up and down, circling the driver persuading him to take us all to Leb'non. Then whispering to me 'Don't pay anything', Abonna joined the girls still persuading a not unhappy, if puzzled driver. Finally reaching his purse, Abonna made an amazingly unsuccessful attempt at opening it, giving the driver ample time to refuse payment, which he did. Relieved no doubt, that he wasn't expected to drive to Leb'non after all.

My last look back showed Abonna tenderly holding his wife's arm, helping her over the stones. Not because she needed help, not simply because they were together, but because they were truly *with* each other. The girls, having given up their petition to the driver surrounded them like a protective flotilla. And who knows! One day perhaps they *will* all go to Leb'non, but I wondered if they could have more fun there, than the fun they were having here and now? They were certainly enjoying the anticipation and preparation.

Simple people in simple places, living simply by simply living, as themselves, no disguises. Deeply spiritual, yet deeply living life; they touched again that connecting thread that ran through all people: unspoilt and unsophisticated being the easier to sense and enjoy.

Twice Viewed

'I've got another job – want to come?

'Yes' I said without knowing what.

'We're going to exhume a body – still want to come?'

My curiosity said, 'Yes'.

Alex did odd jobs whenever he could. Mostly they were legal but those that politically were not legal, were certainly human. On a secluded part of the coast, Alex had shown me piles of upturned crudely hewn canoes that had been washed ashore with or without their occupants.

We were in the tiny one-time Portuguese territory of Macau, gateway to mainland China. Early morning the 'gates' would be opened and merchants would stream across with their wares, do business and return. Split snakes lay drying in the sun on the low sea walls amid the clamour and noise of vendors out-shouting each other for custom.

Alex knew well about escape, hardship and violence. He knew it, had seen it, since the age of six, when he saw his parents hanged from the barn rafters. Now, quietly spoken, vegetarian, he couldn't even walk past the abattoir. So...?

He was a good-looking corpse: all his teeth and plenty of ginger hair. Remnants of cloth covered his bones like a second skin. I don't know what I was expecting but whatever it was, I didn't expect him to look so healthy. With all those teeth, he even seemed to be grinning. A fine happy corpse but – how to remove a whole skeleton? But he wasn't whole, as I discovered.

Each bone, correctly in place, was separate, and one by individual one, we dismantled him. Him? What did I mean 'him'. He was evaporating by the bone. There *was* no more 'him'. I was looking at a man that wasn't there. He had dissolved into a collection of bones that we were placing in a straw platter. Bones that only resembled a person when placed in the shape of one; like a piece of paper that can become the value of the currency that is printed on it. How could a whole person reduce to a simple platterful? No, the sight held a deeper reality, even if I wasn't sure exactly what that reality was.

I look again at the bones in the platter, his – no, *the* skull, is still happily grinning. I look at my own hand and try to visualise *my* bones under the skin. I can't. There's no resemblance. But for something un-graspable, intangible, invisible, the essence of life that activates our being, is a mighty and wondrous phenomenon. I didn't feel I was disturbing the dead. The dead were not there, but peacefully, comfortably, 'at home' somewhere else. I was not shocked or horrified as some people may expect, but more wondrous. It reinforced what I already thought while revealing at the same time, a different wearing of a common cloak.

Whatever Alex felt, viewing the scene from his own life and death experiences, he wore a soft, understanding smile at my reaction. We both knew that the time we value life most, is when we're in danger of losing it.

When the reason for this enforced disturbance of earth emerged it was nothing sinister. As mentioned, Macau is small and after ten years, all graveyard residents must be dug up and their remains placed elsewhere. But in this case, the wife could not face exhuming her husband.

I had not met the man or his wife and can't imagine how it might feel to know someone intimately, then see them as I had seen. Perhaps it would have been as painful or horrific as she imagined or equally, she could have experienced a settling reassurance. Or maybe she preferred to remember him as she used to know him. He did not seem as if he had died in pain, but rather peacefully, contentedly. Whatever had happened, her decision was right for *her,* and became a singular experience for me. I imagined her thoughts.

I've said goodbye, come to terms with it. I'm not squeamish, but live through that twice? I can't. I won't.

And with my 'odd-job' friend on hand, she didn't have to.

Jock and Freddie

It would be simple to say 'and as the Himalayas fade away behind me …' but I can't. Because although physically I was walking out of them I was still very much in them, and they in me. The purity of the mountain air, diversity of the elements, the people who lived with and embraced the harshness and tranquillity of their surroundings, had been my close companions; no strangers. Their fresh and dazzling world had been well worth the swollen eyes, cheeks and ankles I now sported, though not a blister had appeared during the trek. Now I was on my way south with some medicine given me by the Dutch Everest Expedition, who it had been my good fortune to meet, for the Salvation Army in Calcutta.

Calcutta was far from being on the same planet. Despite its contrasts, it did really exist, and so did Maj. Gardiner who, among other things, operated a food run for the local people. He suggested I take the medicine to the Army doctor myself and let him look at my eyes at the same time. Prising lids apart with fingers in order to see *was* a bit inconvenient, so I went. The Doctor didn't entirely blame the blizzard over Jun Besi Pass, as I had done. Apparently, I was suffering a vitamin deficiency. Ankles swelled when no longer supported by boot laces, the only thing that had kept them attached to my feet. Crossing and re-crossing a stream many times at the end of the trip, soles and uppers had separated: at each step boots opened their mouths to the sun and spewed water like happy little whales. Soft shoes returned ankles to normal size, despite their strangeness to my feet. Eyes took a bit longer but treatment and rest at the Army hostel was a good re-orientation. Especially re-uniting and re-familiarising myself with simple things not missed when they weren't there, but so enjoyed when they were, like running my legs over smooth cool sheets and feeling their soothing touch against my skin.

Trains rattled and shunted through the night, stopping between 2 a.m. and 4 a.m. The street sleepers, mainly rickshaw wallahs working away from their village homes, slept on the tram lines at night to save their earnings. Then it was back to their villages and families with the money, returning when they needed more. But there were open spaces too and a boulevard of shops.

As my eyes improved, I appreciated being wrapped into the distinctive, striped and colourful skirt of a girl of the Naga Tribe. Certainly a tonic for sore eyes, not only in colour but it lifted my thwarted ambition (caused by explosions and unexpected skirmishings) of visiting the Naga Hills.

As things progressed, I was able to go with Maj. Gardiner on the food run. The healthy and walking came to the food, the others he visited. That the people didn't always co-operate was no surprise, yet expecting this still didn't help me understand. Why, if they needed the food did they sell their tickets, or send children who lost them or dropped the food or had it stolen? Giving only to adults now worked better. Some gave to us, an empty matchbox, piece of coloured cardboard or similar found treasures. Nice thoughts!

One cheery character (with good reason?) lived in the passageway of a brothel. 'Like ya bread and milk don't ya Guv'nor' said Maj. Gardiner, as the old man grinned and buried his face in the large dish. He looked as if he'd still be going strong in a hundred years. 'How do you find the people?' I asked. 'Easy, just come round the back streets at night and there they are'. 'But weren't they suspicious?' 'No, they know me'. Now, I thought but before? Helping people isn't always easy, yet it seemed to be for Maj. Gardiner.

At the end of a mud road lived Jock and Freddie, two lively Anglo-Indians. Both were lepers. Their hands were badly eaten but that didn't curb their humour. They were interested in people, enjoyed chatting and played cards. All food and drink they were careful to put into their own dishes and mugs, even bottled drinks.

On our next visit, they suggested I come without the food run and stay longer. I said I would. Meanwhile there was plenty to catch up with and new fruit to taste. Varieties of lychee, custard apples, chicos, star apples, star fruit, mangostines and the unidentified, even sometimes by the locals. Smouldering ropes, a service to smokers, hung from kiosks for passers-by to light their fat brown bedis.

Time was short. Would it matter if I didn't go back without the run? Excuses crowded in for not keeping my word. But I did.

'I knew you'd come' said a lone Freddie. 'Jock said you wouldn't. They all say they'll come but there's never time.' (inwardly I groaned. Oh if they had known how close it had been!)

'Where *is* Jock?'

'He's gone to a nice place,' said Freddie. I wasn't sure what he meant but whatever had happened he was taking the loss of his friend very well.

'He's a burnt-out case, so he can go into a home. Not me, I'm still active.' He shrugged. Surely I thought, there must be places where both forms are treated or homes that could take Freddie's active leprosy so that he need not be alone.' When Maj. Gardiner came with the food run we could talk about it, but before he'd even got in the door Freddie shouted 'She came, she came' 'Course she did. Said she would didn't I?' And even after he'd left, Freddie was still imitating 'Told you she'd come if she said she would.' Ouch! what a painful thing is a conscience.

Well, there *were* places for Freddie's stage of leprosy but it took money. Relatives? Yes, a nephew who might help but Freddie didn't know where he was.

When I left to go south, it was with leads to the possible whereabouts of Freddie's nephew down to Bombay, plus The Anglo-Indian Association in Bangalore, ex-servicemen's and C.R.O. records, and last places that Freddie could remember anything useful regarding his nephew.

From places searched, nowhere did I get a glimmer of Freddie's nephew, just a plethora of shaking heads.

Delhi had not been far, but with detours, a puncture and a tangle with a procession, it could have been on the moon. But finally we were in the old part of the city. Sleeping figures carpeted the railway station. Colourful floats and stands, seething crowds filled the oil-lamp and candlelight bazaar, I had arrived in Delhi on the eve of the birthday of the last of the ten gurus, Guru Gobind Singh. The eleventh Guru would be Guru Granth Sahib, the Sikh Holy Book. Shish Gunj was an impressive gurdwara (guru's threshold or Sikh Temple) outlined in coloured lights.

Men, women and children were washing their feet before entering. I took off my shoes and was beckoned into the community atmosphere and buzz of life. This day was certainly special, to the point of making me feel I was back at the Golden Temple of Amritsar, where every day feels special with heightened awareness and energy which was surprisingly relaxing amid so much busy-ness. There, the Temple of marble and gold shines with the love of people who make it a place of great beauty. It lives. It lives from 4 a.m. when the priest takes the Holy Book, Guru Granth Sahib and with closed eyes picks a stanza as a thought for the day, to 11 p.m. when the last poetry is sung. In between, the Temple is a place of social service, a place to meet, to rest, where marriages are arranged, and for some it is home.

Rows of women on the surrounding marble road sat behind troughs of sand cleaning the brass dishes set out with drinking water for anyone thirsting. The giving of food and shelter to travellers had in the past even extended to giving in war. I was shown a bit of history in the form of gold-tipped arrows belonging to a warrior guru. If he wounded his enemy the gold paid for his healing. If he killed him, then the gold paid for his funeral and helped the family. Today, devotees give a percentage of their earnings to charity.

Night throbbed with life more vibrantly than day. Beneath a red velvet and gold tasselled canopy musicians sang and played bongo type drums and harmonium in shifts. Spontaneously groups sang their joy and respect. The Golden Temple itself sits in the middle of the Pool of Nectar (Amritsar) where Guru Ram Das, the 4th Guru, founded it. I felt a little uncomfortable, unworthy, to be invited to join the devotees to the centre sanctuary. This soon changed to a feeling of clean, unsullied reverence, and I happily received in cupped hands, the blessing of sweet things and flowers that had been placed on the Holy Book.

Early morning and the cleaning of the already spotless pavement was a labour of love. A constant flow of people paid their respects, read the thought for the day, sang or read from the Holy Book, lit candles. Some kissed or touched the sacred tree under which one of the Gurus used to sit. An ever-present holiday atmosphere glorified by reverence.

My thoughts returned to Shishgunj in Delhi and its memory provoking similarities. The sun was rising on the great birthday. Guru Gobind Singh heralded a new day of being, doing, living - with flowers, blessings, music, singing and colour. Outside the temple, the market was coming to life. Vendors knelt and bowed toward the temple before selling.

Shamefully, when freely given hospitality as I had received was abused by travellers bringing cigarettes and alcohol over the Guru's Threshold, some temple doors were forced to close to travellers.

From every lead followed, there was still no glimmer of Freddie's nephew. Then, an unexpected spark of hope appeared. It wasn't his nephew but something that might eliminate the need to look further. Maybe I wouldn't need Freddie's relative after all. Someone spoke of a Mr. Mortimer at the British High Commission, in Bombay who had started his own home for people like Freddie with active leprosy.

En route to Bombay in the colourful, noisy, crowded streets that so depicted India, from a once white sports car tied together with string, a Sikh and his daughter offered a lift. To get in I started to untie the door.

'No don't, it'll drop off, climb over'. I did, onto seats disgorging stuffing in every direction. They and the car were a delight.

Daughter flew her own plane, *not* tied together with string and soon after dropping her at the airport she was flying low over us across the road. Both Pappa's hands came off the wheel to wave back. He was a religious man – perhaps he had to be – but philosophical and practical too.

'If I am poor, I cannot give. So I stay rich. I owe it to the poor. How else can I give? If I am poor, who will help me? Certainly not the poor and I must always help others because I don't know who helped me in a past life. Then turning to me said 'Maybe you in a previous life helped me' for he was certain that my western birth was a rebirth and I was now returning home. He even suggested a male Saint that I might have been in a previous reincarnation. I was intrigued that he had no hesitation in a crossover of gender in rebirth. That had never occurred to me. I was wondrous at the thought: wondrous too that he thought nothing of it at all. He was simply offering, as he saw me, an open opinion unhindered by ego.

He was right of course, in that so much giving had to be supplied somehow and I felt privileged to be included in the many gifts which at that moment gave every state or condition a place in the wide scheme of things. And in that scheme there was I knew, a place for Freddie, which I hoped he would soon be sharing in.

My benefactor departed, leaving a space, but with lots of thought to fill it.

When I caught up with Mr. Mortimer, troublesome doubts lurked. Terrific I thought but he won't have room. Wrong, he did. Too costly then? Wrong again. It wouldn't cost Freddie anything. All he had to do was get himself down there and I knew Maj. Gardiner would take care of that. I was thrilled with the news and wrote immediately. Perhaps I could meet them here and see Freddie settled in. Meanwhile, I helped at the Salvation Army Home: playing with the children in the large ground, doing a bit of gardening and checking bunches of safety pins the children had graded.

Despite the many different Indian languages the children spoke, like children everywhere, they had no trouble communicating or playing with each other. Orphans, vagrants, petty thieves, runaways from harsh home or husband. A few were abandoned as babies but most were sent by the court. The Indian Major in charge had the patience of a swami. She probably was one. A lesson to me for the patience I would be needing, to wait for news of Freddie.

If its two things India is not short of its population and celebration. And the next to come was the festivity of Founder teacher Guru Nanak's birthday. The Sikhs went round all day with fried things and sherbet drinks which we prepared and handed out. It was an age before open eager mouths were satisfied, but for as long as the children wanted, the Sikhs would give. Giving was so much part of their religion all year round, but on a special birthday? Wow!

When the S.A. Colonel came, there was more feasting. Sitting cross-legged on mats behind banana leaf platters we ate with fingers from disposable leaf plates: no washing up, and suckable, re-usable fingers. What better manner could there be?

Bombay I realised, led by the Sikh gurus, had instigated a good disguise for the anxiety of waiting for news from Calcutta of Freddie. Would it ever come? Patience. But time past and I decided to move on to the one-time Portuguese territory of Goa.

Goa was a delight. It melted through me. Then from a dark and stormy Coleem, inland and south to Bangalore, where I still might have news of Freddie or even his nephew at the Anglo Indian Association.

The further south I went, the better was the attitude of the men. The difference between north and south was marked. There were even family restaurants where one could eat without being stared at, poked or followed. They also didn't intimidate in groups and where there *was* the odd nuisance, the police intervened - refreshingly on my side.

Then suddenly at a sight before me, in a dip, I stopped dead. Nothing to do with Freddie but, a circus I had given up ever finding. I had met the sister of one of the artists way back but we never did manage to be in the same place at the same time. Now here she was, what a reunion this looked like being. The Company was about to leave Bangalore for Madras and hopefully I could see Freddie settled before going with them. What a wonderful parting gift that would be. Perhaps Freddie was already settled and Maj. Gardiner had arrived with him without writing first. Via Poste Restante I at last received the long-awaited letter from Calcutta. I was thrilled and tore at it frantically.

My elation was shot-down on the instant. I couldn't believe what I was reading. Freddie was dead. Starved himself to death. "We must not blame ourselves. We did all we could" wrote Maj. G. who every day had brought food to him, stayed and talked with him, but every day it was left, he wouldn't eat. Just kept saying 'my number's up guv'nor.'

So much giving and Freddie hadn't been able to partake. Freddie had stopped receiving perhaps because he couldn't believe there was anything to receive. But Freddie, if you had only given yourself the chance to find out before making such a final decision. But maybe you *had* given yourself that time: time enough to decide you wanted to die in the place you had shared with Jock and thought of as home. To wrap yourself in all you had done and enjoyed together, taking the memories with you in your own time.

Who can know what you were ready for? Perhaps Jock was ready for new people and surroundings. Whereas you were as complete and as close to Jock where you were as you would have been anywhere else, if you could not stay together. But who can know what anyone's final thoughts or feelings may be. It's everyone's personal mystery. A path that no-one else can know or take for them.

The Burrha Roti, never called the Big Top, came down and it too breathed its last before moving on to Madras.

A Poor Man's Geisha

At the moment I was working as secretary to the editor of a bilingual magazine. The Japanese secretary to the Japanese editor taught me ikebana and words of Japanese to answer the telephone, though bowing and smiling to visitors seemed more important than words, and a good start. One visitor, Mr. F. a local politician, asked through my boss, if I would 'pour tea', at a religious-political gathering. I visualised the gliding graciousness of a petite kimono-clad Japanese, effortlessly performing every movement with grace and smooth perfection.

So why, I wondered, had he asked *me*? They couldn't afford the real thing perhaps? I wasn't even Japanese, and acquainted with the formality, rules and etiquette which are intrinsic to the Japanese way of life. It naturally followed that tea serving, even at a non-tea-ceremony, would have some expected form. All I had to do was ask. I did. Unfortunately, answers were not so easily forthcoming. The editor's response, 'You'll be told at the time,' was equally unenlightening. It all sounded dangerously last-minute, but perhaps it would be simpler and more obvious 'at the time'.

The meeting was to be held in a Shinto Shrine and when the day arrived, I was still no wiser as to what exactly was expected of me, apart of course from 'pour tea'. A few early guests were already present when I arrived. I was glad to see that Mr. F. was one of them. Now for some instruction.

A nasty feeling grabbed the pit of my stomach as it became clear that Mr. F. spoke very little English. English that consisted entirely of the two words 'pour tea'. It was all I was going to get. From here on, I was on my own.

More guests arrived and sat on cushions placed around a vast square low table. Its vastness was to present a number of difficulties. The first presented itself right now. The tea things were all in the middle of the table. Obviously placed so as to be pleasingly aesthetic to the senses. Though to mine, t'was a sight most disturbing. Did I prostrate myself across the table and make a quick grab? Or should I cut a quick dash to the centre, plant feet firmly, and serve from there? Certainly easier to reach the guests from centre table, though unlikely that either count would be appropriate. But what alternative was there?

I looked at cups and pot. Cups and pot looked back. What did I expect, a talking pot? However, my gaze did produce a Mr. Yamamoto who united tea things with pourer. He had quite a reach. The tea and hot water were already there. Relief. Things were looking up. All I had to do was add the water. But aware of how conscious the Japanese are of the right and wrong way of doing things – right gift, right bow, now the tea was made how to serve it? Did I pour and serve each cup separately, or pour the lot and hope the last ones didn't get cold? A little knowledge is a worrying thing. If the Zen tea ceremony (which this, need I say, was not) was designed to bring peace of mind and Zen Buddhism to give beauty and significance to everyday chores, clearly I was a long way off course. I decided to pour all the cups and start serving from those around me, outward. This I soon discovered called for well-oiled knees and steady hold on handle-less cups to ensure Japanese green tea did not reach honourable guest before cup. Not forgetting of course, to offer the cup with both hands and the customary bow and smile. The table was definitely enlarging itself, and sock-clad feet on slippery cushions and tatami[12] make worthy challenge. Eventually, the last few miles to the final guest were covered.

The next stage, I knew, was to make sure that no cup was ever allowed to become empty. Fine, except the cups weren't transparent and bobbing up and down on my knees just didn't feel right. Mentally I found myself chalking up each sip. Then I gave up and let instinct take over. All went well for about an hour, when Mr. F. caught my gaze and jerked his head towards the door. The door told me nothing. Was he perhaps telling me to go home? I half rose, and sank down again. The same injunction. This time we rose together and I saw; Japanese rice and coconut biscuits, dried

---

[12] Long rush type grass, dried, and woven to flooring blocks

persimmons and juice. Divide and serve.

A pastor began speaking as I opened the persimmons. They were wrapped in cellophane. The gentlest action crunched through the Shrine like ice-breakers on the arctic wastes. I gave up trying to be quiet and ripped at the wrapping as if ripping a plaster off a wound. At which point two late arrivals joined us and I went the rounds with the tea-pot once more… and temporarily suspended the meeting.

One of the new arrivals had been passed a cup. As I knelt beside him, pot poised to fill it he reared up on his knees, remonstrated vehemently, snatched pot and flung himself protectively over his own and every other cup within reach. Quite a feat over such a vast expanse of table; at the same time sweeping the pot far from *my* reach. Mr. F. sprang to my defence, adding a second body to the table, as he threw himself over man who snatched pot. In seconds, a peaceful Japanese Shrine had become a scene from a Chicago shootout, except I didn't understand a word. From the same very un-Japanese position, Mr. F. pointed to me, the opposition and the pot, and machine-gun fashion rattled off a flow of Japanese.

This had a sudden and disarming effect upon my assailant; disarmed him of the pot anyway, which he had since re-hoisted and was waving in the air. Graciously, he surrendered his weapon to me with a bow and a smile. And as if nothing had happened…

had it? the injunction 'Pour tea' and meeting, were resumed.

Phew! No wonder the Geisha trains from childhood. Imagine contending with musical instruments, tea ceremony, dancing, fan movements, flower arranging and conversation – to order. I couldn't even 'pour tea' without starting a punch-up: and with no idea why or how? Still, I knew that at least two of the men were representatives in Japan for the Society of World Peace, so I felt on reasonably safe ground.

When the meeting came to a close, Mr. Yamamoto introduced me to the guest speaker who wished to apologise to me. Apologise? Why? Piecing bits together through Mr. Yamamoto, the speaker had mistaken me for a Japanese and thought I might have been insulted. Insulted? I couldn't have been more delighted. What a compliment! Short, with dark eyes and hair padded out Japanese style, I had sometimes been taken for Japanese by Americans, but never by a Japanese. Perhaps my ungainly western efforts hadn't been too way out after all - if he really thought that. The men apparently said they had enjoyed my coming, though perhaps they meant, they had enjoyed the novelty.

I was much less successful in trying to find out what had upset honourable guest who snatched pot. 'Yes,' he was an old-fashioned Japanese, who regarded me as a guest and could not therefore allow himself to be served by me, and 'Yes,' he was a traditional Japanese, who would expect to be served by a woman. 'Yes' can mean anything, even 'no' which is never used. Too harsh. So 'yes' is a kind of oriental 'Yes, we have no bananas'.

Following my great 'pour tea' escapade, purely for my own interest, I went to a traditional Japanese lady which – had I done so in the first place, might have saved honourable face – to learn how things *should* be done. Kosakosan, explained that the man of highest rank, who should always be served first, sits, in typical Japanese room, by the Tokonoma post.[13] Mmh!

'Lower ranking men sit towards shoji entrance. Every cup of tea must be made equally mild.' Drawing diagrams of each step, Kosakosan showed how a little is poured into each cup, then start again, three times, before serving.

'This is the secret. How to make every cup taste so good, and *smile*.' I got the impression that if the roof fell in, or I broke someone's leg, and I *smiled*, then in Japanese eyes, the evening would have been a success.

As I said, this was for my own interest. I wasn't expecting to be asked again. In fact, I was astonished when a second invite arrived. This time from Mr. Yamamoto and Mr. F. together, 'Please to

---

[13] The single post of the shallow corner platform where either a scroll painting hangs or some art form is displayed, such as a sculpture depicting nature, or ikebana

serve green tea and Shirashi-sushi.' Mr. Yamamoto was finding his English in leaps and bounds? Feeling more relaxed now, I agreed.

The tea things were within easy reach. The raw fish spread over rice in round lacquer boxes served with ginger, horseradish and soy sauce, arrived. I couldn't go wrong. Mr. F. and Mr. Yamamoto were the only familiar faces but as things went so smoothly, I was able to eat with them. Yes, a box had been ordered for me also. When all were served, and feeling content and comfortable, I picked up my chopsticks.

Mr. Yamamoto spoke to me directly, from the other side of the table. 'You are famous in the market.' Everyone stopped to listen. 'You buy so much.' It seemed they had been discussing the fact that Japanese housewife trips out daily to shop, whereas the 'geijin'[14] bought more than a housewife with a family to feed. Chopsticks poised, my appetite deserted me. I replaced them.

'Er, oh not so often of course' beamed Mr. Yamamoto, 'But *so* much more.'

Suddenly feeling like a graceless glutton, I did the only thing possible. I smiled. *Then* picked up my chopsticks.

---

[14] Foreigner

Serendipity and the Heike Clan

To find a Clan you have set out to find is an achievement. To find a Clan you were not looking for, didn't know existed or had ever been lost, is a revelation. But to start at the beginning.

Two stops from Tokyo-Ikkebukuro, was the student village of Ekoda. A nine tatami mat room there, supplied by a small team I had joined, producing a bi-lingual magazine, became my home. The chance to supplement the pocket money received from this work, came from an unexpected quarter; a Shinjuku coffee shop, where I was 'discovered' by a film scout looking for a 'geigin'. Foreign faces were scarce then but it was something I could definitely supply for TV plays and films.

'Extra' work was interesting: getting to a studio or location at the required time was a problem. How to wake up in the dark early hours, get up and stay up?

Ekoda had many street vendors of tasty, wholesome food that changed with the seasons. The vendor of bamboo washing poles could be heard crying his wares through the narrow streets and the politely termed 'Japanese perfume' men – who syphoned off the pit-toilets announced themselves with wheels, pipes and other appropriate equipment. As with everything the Japanese did, the process was clean and effective despite how it may sound. Though I knew of no Japanese who had it in their tea, milk was delivered – in the dark early hours. Could this be the answer?

Student Iwashita, smiling behind the milk bottles was willing to make sure I was awake when I ought to be. Thus, we both did our various jobs, while getting to know each other through English conversation sessions (though his English was already good) and mutual friends. It was through one of these friends that I became aware of Iwashita's island home.

The remarkable thing to me was that the entire island of Kodakarajima, consisted of one family – Iwashita's family. I was intrigued, but to him it was just home. A home he saw as no different to the Buddhist, Christian or Shinto events we shared. The latter, not only in Shinto temples but as the spiritual basis of Sumo. Nothing was more this or that, everything was simply what it was. With open involvement, we had participated with the same respect, interest and meaning in every form of worship.

It was with eager excitement that I agreed to the idea of visiting Iwashita's home when he next went. What an invitation! Though it wasn't that simple to get started. At first we travelled together, then apart, then together, while waiting for a convenient time for both of us to visit his island home in the

Ryukus. But with so many things to do and see on the journey south from Tokyo, and with so many comings and goings between us, getting there would happen when we each arrived.

There was one boat a week to Kodakarajima from Kagoshima in the south of Kyushu. Somewhere in Kyushu, the southernmost of the four main islands that comprise the body of Japan, I had lost a day. The boat was leaving in half an hour. Along with chickens and a cow I went aboard. On deck, tatami mats and head/neck boards were neatly placed for sleeping. The chickens and cow were accommodated below.

En route south to Kagoshima Port, Iwashita had needed to rest and we planned to meet later. I am lucky in that I rarely get sick but now it was my turn to feel something 'not quite right'. Stretched out on deck, I felt helpless to move. I needed to drink but any effort was too much. My body had given up. Not that I was sea-sick, just sick.

Towards the end of the second day, through swollen eyes, I noticed peaches and little portions of food beside me placed by thoughtful Japanese. I sat up to acknowledge them and found smiling faces nodding encouragement. Perhaps I should show my appreciation and eat. It was a waste of good food; instantly it went to the sea.

The fish weren't having a good time either. The deck was slippery with blood and several times had to be hosed down. With weighted line and hook (no rod) let out from the stern, the men hauled in great, powerful sea 'monsters' that propelled themselves about the deck on wildly beating tail and fin. Fanged snouts, broad, flat heads, sharp pointed noses, slit and bulging eyes, rows of saw-edged teeth, all as vicious looking as others were small and delicate. The jumping slap, slap, slapping on deck was endless.

We arrived at 11 p.m. in a night shot with stars lower, brighter, bigger and stiller than I had ever seen. A thick milky way was a 'frosty' glow. The plough, low on the horizon, tipped the silhouetted island hilltops. Shooting and falling stars sped across worlds. I was enchanted, wrapped in a world I had not seen before; partially familiar but so low around me that I felt part of the cosmos itself. It was tangible.

We anchored out. A small boat bounced over the waves and came alongside. A fit and smiling Iwashita, was in it. Many hands from the small boat took off boxes, cylinders, bundles and the chickens. The cow had gone ashore on a previous island and the chickens were replaced with three reluctant goats. Above the din and bouncing boats Iwashita called:

'Have you seen the stars?'

'Seen them! I was about to pick one'. Low, large and enveloping, they hung ripe for the taking.

On the shore about thirty or so people waited with lamps.

'Nobody in the village now. All here' confided Iwashita. Curious they flashed their lamps over me. My visit must have been as strange to them as their night sky wonder was to me.

'Maybe a foreigner came to the island before but long time ago. No-one can remember for sure. But, if you are not the first, then you *are* the first woman'. Iwashita had a lot of translating to do and his family were losing no time.

We followed a grassy path through a strong smell of sulphur to a group of wood and bamboo houses. In one of them I met sister Micahco, brother Liu, and mumma and pappa Iwashita. We talked by the dim, fluctuating light of... not lamps, but a generator that operated for about three hours each night.

Despite the late hour, mumma had prepared noodles. I still wasn't up to eating but I could just make out, in a dim corner, the family altar. Already well stocked with bottles containing sake, I was to get used to mumma adding her own offering. In little cups she placed noodles from the family meal in front of the altar, then returned them to the rest of the meal. A blessing to the past, given back to the present? But what was their past? Even the name of Kodakarajima hinted at mystery and intrigue, meaning as it did 'Little Treasure Island'.

With bedding spread around the floor, we

prepared for sleep. I had no idea what, but at that point Mumma made a discovery: came exclamations and examinations of my back, which had suddenly become a point of interest to everyone. Seems that as well as sore eyes and puffy cheeks, my back sported a close-knit rash.

'Back stars' quipped Iwashita, in humorous pun on my name. His refreshingly quick and unexpected wit was always a fun surprise. More so perhaps because it was humour from a language not his own.

With the sliding front of the house open, the night had many voices.

Come morning sun and breakfast, I was eager to get to grips with this unique island. Steam jets rose from clusters of grey bubbling sulphur springs that cratered the earth in varying degrees of heat – the source of the sulphur we had passed through the night before. The hot putty-like mud that surrounded each of them sank underfoot. At one fiercely churning pool that boiled hypnotically, Iwashita said darkly, 'Fall in, then die'.

Mumma and Pappa layed out palm fronds to dry which later would be made into fans. These, along with rock plants, would be sold in Kagoshima. Everyone was busy in a relaxed sort of way. Weaving of all kinds, including strips of bamboo to make baskets for carrying fish, vegetables and anything that needed carrying.

When they grew their own tatami, pappa wove mats and nailed them to the wood blocks for flooring. He still did, only now they bought tatami. Salt too was bought, where once they made it by boiling sea water for hours, but sugar still came from island sugar cane. When breeding was good, they sold cows. Though predominantly still self-supporting, they sold more now because they bought more.

Time was nowhere. Days blended into it and disappeared. Little Treasure Island fascinated me, especially the families. All mumma's children had been born on the island, the older women acting as midwives, but now, that too was changing as some of the younger wives chose to go to Kagoshima or Amami Oshima to give birth. The children readily accepted me except for one puzzled little girl. She whispered something to Iwashita who fell about laughing. When he'd recovered, he said. 'She ask me how you have grown so big without learning to talk. Everyone knows only babies can't speak Japanese'. Since baby talk and Japanese were the only two sounds she knew, the sounds I was making *could* only be baby talk, since they weren't Japanese: a perfect piece of logic.

Getting *around* the island took a mere half an hour non-stop; only there always was something to stop for. Another simple shrine with twig torii, a grave marked by stone piles, sake cups and bottles, a new rock formation. Getting to *know* the island, including its history, would take longer.

Going to a Post Office is not unusual, but the one here was. It must be the smallest in the world. A 6"x 4"x 2" metal box containing stamps. The person taking letters to and from the boat had the title 'postman'. No clutter. Just what was needed for the job. A stamp.

A more detailed and precise skill was performed just as simply. During the turmoil of scrambling goats and bobbing boats my watch had got torn from my wrist, the pin lost. Sayigi, one of Iwashita's eleven brothers and sisters, took it, looked closely at it and got to work. Shaping and filing, testing and smoothing a piece of metal, he worked single-mindedly till it matched the other pin perfectly. My watch was whole again. Sayigi's pleasure and obvious satisfaction at making things so precisely was a double credit to his one eye. Sayigi also cut hair.

TV being as natural as breathing to the Japanese, the island had three sets – all showing the same 'noisy snow'. For the same reason, no reception, the one dusty telephone had never been in use. But such things had little place here and were not missed. The three classroom school, closed now for summer, was good for playing games.

There were three chiefs, in name only, though no-one seemed to know who they were. People managed themselves, and why not? They were all the same family. Yet, for that very reason, one might expect an arbiter to be necessary. But this family was practical, cohesive and clearly survivors. Everything was open and belongings were safe anywhere.

In fact, the only thief on the island was me. On one of my discovery walks around new sulphur springs and shrines was - was that a coconut? Strange, as there were no coconut palms on the island, so...! I picked it up, took it back and curious we broke it open. It was bad.

'All the same' said Iwashita, 'Find something, leave it. Maybe belong to someone'. It did. Delighted when it was washed ashore, finder/owner put it aside to collect later. A puzzled and not so delighted owner returned to the village pondering mystic disappearance of coconut. Hmmm. Everything safe on the island, except from me. I confessed my misdemeanour to him and saw things differently thereafter.

When she wasn't weaving, Micahco took me to her favourite high spots on the island. Alone and high up, we looked down on the sea, the cows, thin wavy sheets of lacework rock and massive palm type flowers growing low to the ground. But the sweetest of all, we could feel a relieving cool breeze. 'Artsui' was on everyone's lips and in everyone's hand a towel to dab our leaking skins.

There were few people working the fields now despite there's always something to be done on the land - the ever moving time measurement. What better non-winding time-piece than the sowing, growing, harvesting seasons and possibly the elements? Any other kind of clock was superfluous. Body clocks gave hunger/eating time, thirst gave drinking time, sunset/dusk proclaimed the visual coming of night, body clock gave tiredness, the time to sleep and when replete, it rang the body clock's alarm to wake.

However, fishing was everyone's all-time harvest. One night our supper was caught by a twelve-year-old and once we had lobster for breakfast. Liu caught a fish, but had eaten half of it before reaching home. Holding it up, mumma laughingly declared 'Humbum Sashimi'. Well 'half' was better than nothing. In Pappa's younger days he made his own harpoons for catching shark.

Though hot, it was good sometimes to bathe in the hot springs. Micahco took me to the springs that were temperature safe. Not the 'Fall in. Then die' kind.

Though nothing was fenced off, out or in, somehow we never clashed with the boys, but this was only respect, and not politeness because I was western. The attitude of the Japanese to sex is wonderfully refreshing, open and natural. Non-prudish and never embarrassing.

But my greatest pleasure was sea-swimming amid life and beauty. Home-made goggles: shaped glass fixed into wood with wax, and completely waterproof, brought our ocean world closer. And there was always something new. Coral gardens, discreet and startling colours, hideaway homes of the flimsy wavering fin, the sudden marble eye, sharply darting bodies, fluorescent, transparent and electric. Oh to be an amphibian and breathe underwater. Even above the surface by the shore, huge-headed sea fish stared out of water holes and long skinny banded sea snakes slopped up from the sea fungus to flop on the coral shelves. A quick breath, then once more into the depths to greet mightily toothful and bristling creatures, warlike species in 'armour plating' and sometimes - each other!

Nobody swam alone. It was 'Abunai'. I never knew why. Undercurrents, poisonous sea snakes or seaweed? I heard 'Abunai' so often that 'Dangerous', lost much of its meaning. Though the one place the family were absolutely definite about my not going into, I was more than glad to comply with; the caves. In fact I hadn't seen any but they were home to serpents with a venom that could kill. A cobra-like species of snake. Here, 'Abunai' was more of an understatement.

Liu had learned to say 'Let's go' so that often I didn't know where to or what for, till we arrived. Following a 'Let's go' one night, Mumma was pulling me back with some forceful 'Abunai'. Iwashita said 'Come anyway'.

They were going lobster fishing and the sharp rocks I knew cut rubber soles to pieces. The slightest touch on skin made an 'abunai' nasty mess. But was that mumma's only fear? Were there more creatures I didn't know about?

By lamplight, we tied bait into each glassy waterhole and later returned for the catch. Liu handed me a lobster to carry back. When we got home, it was dead. I felt like a murderer and couldn't eat it. This was totally illogical. Ridiculous. Fish was our main food. I like fish. I eat fish. Hadn't we once had lobster for breakfast? I'd enjoyed it. Not as a luxury, but as the nourishment the sea provided for us. So why not now? Could the fact that it had died in *my* hand have made that much difference? How stupid, as well as hypocritical. But it stayed uneaten by me. Catching crabs was something else I needed to get used to. Iwashita pieced their crusty backs and I put them in the basket. What a dilemma to work through! Though before the night was out, I was to learn of another's dilemma.

That night Liu entertained with impersonations of villagers dancing in their own and different styles. Iwashita regaled us with stories of houses that were haunted by the spirits of the people who had died there. And Pappa intrigued us, with tales of 'Kappa': a creature that he and other men had seen. Kappa had the front and back of a turtle, a half human face, and it walked upright on two legs. To add to this precise and powerful description, Iwashita translated that Kappa had something 'dishlike' on its head. About the size of a small man, kappa comes to boats at night and eats the fish. There was no record of kappa eating humans, only fish.

A good story I thought, for someone returning with a poor catch, 'But darling, the Kappas came', but 'No'. Kappa was real. Kappa lived. It was no convenient creation.

At this point, I am eager to freeze the family on the island for a flexible moment of time while we look into the future, where much later I was astonished to discover by chance, a written record of the existence of Kappa. Kappa had been seen and accepted in other places, different in form, characteristics and nature but still referred to as 'kappa'. The written version also explained Iwashita's addition to the island Kappa of something dish-like on its head.

The dish contains the Elixir of life which Kappa carries, so bow. And when Kappa returns the bow, as he must, or lose face, he will lose the Elixir, and still lose face. Useful and interesting to know, had I been lucky enough to have such an encounter, and things got a bit out of hand. But what a dilemma for Kappa. Either way he loses face and goes away in shame. No wonder he is shy to be seen.

What amazed me, was that Kappa was a recorded and accepted mythical creature, yet here on the island, I was hearing about it first hand from the lips of people who had never left their island home, and who could never have read about it. Pappa's knowledge was what he and the others had experienced personally. Were they the originators then of the sighting? If so, how was it recorded? Or was the creature more widespread than this island? In which case, is it a myth seeing that different people in different places had seen the same thing independently?

But to return through time to the island party.

We talked of all kinds of things including a species of crab that inhabited these waters. It was never caught, and if caught by accident, it was always thrown back. It thrived through natural selection. The crab was considered sacred because it had the markings of a human face on its back. When first caught, fishermen threw it back because it was different and they were wary of it. Thus, the human face crab was safe to prosper and increase to become a prevalent sacred species. Did Kappa survive the same way, an unexplained form that appeared without known reason? Best avoided but if encountered, then left alone to thrive unharmed? Its original birth was tantalising.

Getting the island's history was still as tantalising but now Iwashita revealed that about 800 years ago when many Clans in Japan were warring, some people fled in a boat and were shipwrecked here. They found fresh water from a well, where it still comes from today, liked the island and stayed. At first they lived in caves, the same caves now inhabited by 'harbu' the 'hevvi' with the venom that can kill. Later the people built houses, fished and planted.

Mumma Iwashita also had a story to tell. A story concerning some bad men who came to steal from neighbouring Treasure Island. The islanders killed one of them and the rest fled. Since any island here was itself a treasure, I wondered what they expected to find worth stealing. 'Gold' translated Iwashita 'Not much and now finished. That's why it's called Takara-jima – Treasure Island. This is Ko-dakara-jima – Little Treasure Island. And yes' he laughed 'With "ko" the T becomes, d'.

The quantity of pumice washed up on the shore brought forth knowledge of a nearby volcanic island. The more I listened the more I wanted to know. The island had its own Shaman, a Priestess, and from there it was said that one can sometimes hear the voice of a drowned princess calling to her lost lover.

During the turbulent days of clan warfare, the princess's lover was lost at sea. Desperate to find him, she would not give up her search. Eventually, exhausted, she tragically drowned in her attempt to find him. Still at times, she can be seen striving to reach him and her voice can be heard calling to him.

When the frothy white sea raged and flew, and nature's high-tuned voices echoed in eerie cacophony from the ocean depths, to clash with the winds fury above, she could well be part of the brilliant, yet misty tracery.

These were lazy days that gave significance and pleasure to the simplest act, from bringing in the fish drying on the rocks when the sun sank into the ocean; chasing off the wee beasties that had found it during the day, to coaxing crops from the ground, or splashing in the sun's colourful liquid as it plunged rapidly into the sea. But don't stand under the 'ciquada' tree with unblocked ears. The shrill, piercing ringing from so many vibrating bodies attacked without mercy. They also joined the other flying, crawling creatures in the house despite bowls of water spread around to invite suicide. But in the tree, they became chicken 'obento'. Sayigi made banana leaf funnels, fixed them to the top of a bamboo pike, then up into the branches with it. The insects fell into the 'death-tube' and were gobbled immediately from the funnels by the chickens. So much vibration instantly cut short in the stillness of death – till life started up again, as their piercing ringing tones testified from the tree.

It was good there were no electronic sounds from TV or telephone. They wouldn't have stood a chance against the ciquadas. Not that there was a need for such things: too much life in the living to attend to, interest in each other and enthusiasm in working together was enough. Anything else would be an unnecessary substitute.

Japan, Land of the Bath, had offered many varieties and elements to enjoy on the mainland, including a memorable sand bath, the only one of its kind left, I was told. Memorable it certainly was but now I was about to be given the rarest of baths by Micahco. I followed as she beckoned me to the chicken enclosure. With the chickens all outside of it, we had the place to ourselves. I had no idea what to expect but knew it wouldn't be long before I found out. Micahco was busy making preparations. When she was ready, I was left in no doubt.

First one near scalding bucket of water came my way, followed swiftly by a second and a third, at me and over me until I was 'done', that is, glowing and steaming fit to fuse. Then zealously she got to work on every inch of my body with two fingers, rubbing deeply and vigorously. Heat and rub was the prescribed order. From her expression and exclamations, it was clear she disapproved of the condition of my body. Shaking her head in disbelief she kept repeating 'Empai, empai' – full, full. A fact that spurred her on with even greater zeal, if that were possible. Micahco certainly didn't run out of steam even though it seemed I had most of it. Already I looked like something boiled and covered in desiccated coconut. Except for the steam, I was the perfect stand-in for a light-house. In the sand bath my arms had been pounding, and everything throbbed till I thought my hands would burst and fly off out of the sand. This bath was less severe and had a good balance of overall cleansing.

I don't remember how long the whole process took but it was certainly thorough. A final bucket of water came my way that left me glowing like an overcooked lobster at melting point. Without doubt, I was tingly clean, having been relieved of an outer layer (or more?) of skin and a deal of uric acid. I knew she was asking how long since I was last cleansed. I hadn't the face to tell her 'never', but it was certainly far too good to have only once in a lifetime. A pity the West isn't as massage and bath conscious, but what an experience to have had even once!

To build a wall for a new cow pond, nearly everyone turned out. There was plenty to do for everyone from collecting wood for morning brew up drunk with sato, the familiar brown sweet substance derived from sugar cane, to getting buckets of water to mix the filler that was to be poured between the double wood walls. Then we became a human conveyor belt or 'chain gang', passing buckets and anything needed up ramps and along planks, in humorous, vocal rhythm one to the other. So far we had avoided the catastrophe that Iwashita said might happen, 'Call me Iwashita on my island and everyone will answer', but with first names for everyone else it was simple. Except that everyone had learnt to say 'Yes' and did, at the drop of an 'Iwashita'. All of which became part of the working fun which continued till lunch time. By which time I'd learnt that though a western 'I' or 'Me' is indicated by pointing to the chest, a Nihon 'Watashi' is indicated by pointing to the nose. And why not?

Lunch of fish, seaweed and vegetables had been keeping cool beneath the shade of rocks. Now it was pulled out to make a welcome spread. We put the final touches to the wall before enjoying juicy watermelon; just before little bursts of rain began to relieve the heat.

Several days later, the sea was thunder on the shore. Typhoons were brewing. 'Here they start' warned Iwashita in his dark 'fall in, then die' voice.

Evening and the spray greeted us a long way inland. What a sight! The violence was terrifying. Huge waves broke in threatening rhythm. A plateau of craggy rocks round one of the deep inland pools was a mass of threshing foam. A brief shaft of sunlight struck the next wave, tracing gold upon white. An uninhabited island off-shore was 'alight' with waves that reared, folded and broke high against the wind. The air was charged with a vibrant energy.

White 'steam-engines' attacked our island on waves turned by a giant plough. Sometimes the intensity of white lit up the entire ocean. The plateau was now a frothy, boiling eruption from the white heat of the earth's core. Sudsy streams flowed down from the black rock headlands.

'Did you before see like this? asked Iwashita, as he stood with me in my transfixed wonder.

'Never', I breathed.

'I am used to seeing, when small, but I am still surprised. But this is another-world-island with many strange things, like primitive. Do you want to see?'

'Yes' I said, without knowing what. The island had much to offer that continued to expand my limited knowledge of this wondrous planet Earth.

'Alright, but don't touch. Very dangerous. It's an animal'.

I followed Iwashita to the Banyan tree, the one with the dangling rope-like branches which we swung on: but not tonight. Something beside the playfully rooting 'swing tree' was the point of interest. As we came closer, the 'something' appeared to be a large wide drum. Inside was something far from playful. Perhaps because Iwashita had said it was an animal I had expected to see something furry. Inside was an unbelievably monstrous crustacean, as close to any prehistoric creature as I was likely to see outside of a horror film. It was confined to the drum by a rope slipped around its body. No mean achievement in itself and presumably done from a safe distance with a pole or two.

'Hermit crab' said Iwashita. Hmmh! a hermit crab to me was a little thing that drew in its spiky legs when you picked up its shell.

'Yes, this one too big for hermitage'. Iwashita tapped its armour plating shell with a bamboo pole to show that it didn't need any other shell, it had grown its own. Its body alone was easily two feet across, its jointed legs about a foot long, with the thickest pair of war-like pincers heading the armoury. It must surely have lived many lifetimes to have survived to that size and strength. The Islanders reckoned it to be at least 100 years old, maybe more, but no-one knew for sure.

'Very strong' said Iwashita unnecessarily, as he tapped the shell with the pole. It sounded like a small tank. In confirmation, its weaponry reached out, grabbed the bamboo pole and proceeded to crush and splinter. It held on to its 'prey' and continued to shred and mangle till there was nothing left but fibres.

'If take, not give back', said Iwashita pulling up on the top of the bamboo remnants with all his strength. The creature tenaciously clung on, still grinding, the crab's weight preventing it from being lifted by the pole. What, I wondered, would it do to a human limb? The creature had been found in the undergrowth but where had it been living since then? What if I had met it on my island explorations? A story that your missing arm or foot had been crushed by a crab would be a little hard to swallow. And talking of swallowing, what did this creature eat? Hopefully, just larger portions of what normal sized crabs ate.

Monstrous as it was, I was beginning to feel sorry for this fiercesome creature. Physically it seemed indestructible, but that is not the only thing that builds life force. Since it was assumed he was a 'one off', no mates, or mate, it must surely have been lonely. The thought of being the only one of your species left on the planet! Not that the crab's thought processes worked that way, but it was still an existence unshared and compared to most species, unnatural.

All night the sea crashed, fit to drive the island from the earth's face. Water covered everything but its sound. Next morning all around was a white rage. White, white and unbelievably beautiful. The boats certainly would not come. There had been talk of them coming before but now…? And too, the mysterious creature of the night before had gone and no-one could tell me where or how, or what had happened to it. I can't imagine that it escaped yet the thought that it had been killed wasn't comforting, for it wouldn't have died easily.

By evening, the wind was at its fiercest. Darkening skies dropped a sense of foreboding. The ocean hypnotised me. It churned far out as if sea dragons were wrestling in the deep, surfacing only to blow water jets 30 ft high. There were few birds on the island but now even the sea eagles hid.

Nothing deterred the cicadas. The night for the first time was totally black. Amid the high pitched ringing of the cicadas and the roaring, pounding of the elements, I listened intently for the weaving through of an anguished cry. But any princess or kappa would surely be taking refuge in the deep, below the turmoil.

We were lucky; the main force of the typhoon by-passed us during the night. Iwashita warned 'Now the rains have come, more snakes go walking' and they did. Later, in answer to father's shouts of 'Jun, Jun', my island name, 'Hevvi, Harbu hevvi', I went outside. A group of people were slaughtering a snake. A more erudite hevvi was killed in the school which was closed now for the summer. But generally hevvis and humans didn't encroach upon each others' territory, a fact fancifully, put down to my not having disturbed the serpents caves!

For yet another night, we slid the shutters early. The storm lasted through the night and brought a cooler morning. Something odd had happened during the night. The island had changed shape. The fiercest of the typhoon had driven great boulders inland This made the coastline too shallow for even a tiny outboard. Lots of activity followed, mostly underwater, in the fun-work of diving down and shifting the boulders by hand. For the ones that were too huge to be moved despite so many willing hands, a winch creaked into play. Finally, we had pushed and hauled the sea-bed back to its former shape and navigational depth.

It was a few days later when a 'New rice' festival revealed 'hidden treasure' that completed the islanders' unique and exciting history. A history, like the Clan themselves, that I only discovered by chance. The treasure of this little island was not gold but the people. Certainly they were gold as people, but more, they *were* their own history, which made them treasure twice over.

The path to the beach followed a shady walk through palms till the smooth rock either side met overhead in wedge-shaped arches. We took off zorii and geita but sturdy leather shoes I noticed, could stay on. The way opened out: we had arrived. Like all island shrines, here was a kennel-like wooden shape, side on, with shells, sake cups (though not always) plus the branch Torii: which combines nature with ancestor worship in Shintoism.

Priest Iwashita wore a long white coarse robe and carried the traditional 'stick'. Here in humble dress in a simple rock setting, the giving of thanks was about to begin. We stood around the altar and watched Priest Iwashita take palm leaves and a tray of new rice balls up to the altar in the rocks. He stood back, knelt for a moment, blessed the food, then brought it down again.

'Now everybody pray' whispered Iwashita

We clapped twice, bowed in silent prayer for a moment, then sat on the hicklety-picklety rocks to eat the new rice. Could this be the shortest 'Thanks' for harvest ever offered?

When we returned, I asked about the shoes and the priest: how had he become a priest? – Ordination didn't seem relevant or even appropriate. It wasn't. His priesthood was as simple as the service. He was a priest because his father and grandfather had been before him, back to the Heike Clan. What did he say? The Heike Clan!? How was that possible? History said the Heike Clan was wiped out. Everyone drowned. And here were those very people around me, speaking as if their survival was the most natural thing in the world, and needed no explanation.

As for the shoes – the family still revered the God of their Heike ancestors, who was a strong god, and liked walking. Flimsy sandals are not good for striding out, so rather than offend him they are removed when in his presence. Strong shoes, made him happy and could be kept on.

Was I really in the midst of a family descended from the sole survivors of the Heike Clan! And if so, how could this part of their history emerge in such an unassuming manner, giving mind exploding answers to the simplest of questions.

This was not only another-world-Island, it was another-time-Island.[15]

The unexpected revelation of this unwritten history stayed with me. Stories that Iwashita had told me now made a different sense. He had explained about the shipwreck on the island about 800 years ago when clans were warring, how they found water from a well, where it still comes from today, survived in caves, fished, built houses and planted. I had no inkling then that he was speaking of their own history, a remnant of the Heiki Clan itself. Living history. We all have a history but this was a unique thread of life, still breathing from something thought to be no longer in existence. And I was living in it.

But next day my thoughts were drawn away by children making paper shapes to be strung on fresh cut bamboo. I had already learnt a lot from stories and was eager to learn about this one. This however was quite different: the story of Tanabata, The Weaver's Star Festival. Legend tells of a sky-dwelling King who lived with his beautiful daughter who spent her days weaving. One day he

---

15 Later I learnt from recorded history that Heike and Genji (sometimes called Taira and Minemoto) had three main battles. In 1159 Genji attempted to wipe out Heiki because he was jealous over his popularity for fighting off pirates. Genji almost succeeded but Heike recovered and conquered Genji. However, in 1185, in a naval battle off Shimonoseki, Heiki was defeated. Nothing is written about the few survivors, their escape in boats, or the Island people, the worthy few now about 30-35 strong. Perhaps today alas, not even that

gave her a holiday which she spent along the river of the Milky Way, where she met a man washing a cow. They fell in love and she stayed with him. The king, anxious for his daughter when she did not return went looking for her. He found her and took her back by force, but she could no longer weave, she could only cry. Finally the king granted her one day a year to visit her lover. Tanabata is kept to celebrate the day when the Weaver Star, Vega, meaning lyre or harp and the Cow Herder Star, Altair, meaning flying eagle come together from across their own sides of the river.

That night they met in secrecy, for the Milky Way was completely hidden. Remembering the huge stars that fell low around me on arrival, I was surprised there were not more stories about the stars: but this was not a Festival unique to the Island. Tanabata was commemorated all over Japan.

Three times the boat ferrying the islands came and went but neither time was it going to Kagoshima. With an extra mouth to feed for so long, Mumma did well on two cylinder gas rings. A fire between stones on the kitchen floor was used mainly for smoking fish or making dofu.

Meanwhile I helped mumma split and shell sago palm seeds and spread them to dry. Their milky juice was starchy and stained our hands white. After crushing, grinding and mixing with wheat, it was fermented to make island mizu. Anywhere else and mizo was fermented soybean. Only difference with the sago, it gave a white pinhead sediment to the soup.

Making dofu (beancurd) was something of a zen discipline in itself; being typical of the care and attention the Japanese give to detail. Patiently Mumma husked the beans and soaked them overnight, the remaining fibres floating to the top.

Next morning, between two large round stones Mumma's strong hands ground the soaked beans, then she poured two parts of water in the top till a frothy cream began to ooze. Then came the rigorous job of straining the last fibres. Mumma Iwashita must surely have had the strength of a Sumo wrestler for she then filled a long cotton bag with fibres and sloshed it from side to side. Then she wrung out the bulging bag, twisting it, till she could tip out the dry fibres into a bucket, which quickly became as full of residue as it had been of beans. Twice more the sediment was watered and wrung out.

'Mendoksai' said Mumma in polite understatement. Since 'Mendoksai' merely meant ' troublesome', I wondered what she really thought, but I had a suspicion that she meant just what she said; with a smile.

After four concentrated hours of straining, watering, sloshing and wringing, the 'milk' was put into an iron pan over a bamboo fire. When it boiled,

Mumma skimmed off the top and added water in blobs. The fire was put out. More pockets of water were added and the fire rekindled. At the water patches, the milk began to curdle. Next step – sink a basket into the liquid, and drain it off over a bucket of whey.

Only water had been used to curdle the milk, but then no yeast had been used to ferment the mizo. When Mumma finally spooned the mixture into a sectioned wooden box lined with a cloth, the whey continued to ooze through the holes. It took yet another hour for the curd to set. We ate the dofu with soy and shark which had been caught the night before with hook and line and weighed about 15 kilos.

Could anything that had taken so long to prepare, take so little time to eat? It was certainly appreciated but so quick to vanish. True Mumma's efforts were practical rather than a formal or traditional discipline despite their warrior background, yet were probably inherent because of it. They lived in the open, close to nature, in their own time and space. There was no-one to keep up with; only what they set themselves. Their striving was basic, and came from inside rather than outside pressure.

When the boat once more returned, yes, it was going to Kagoshima. With me came the generator which had broken down and from another island came two oxen.

In port I packed up a parcel and took it to Kagoshima Post Office. The clerk looked at the address and reluctantly told me there was no such place. I told him I had just come from there. He smiled kindly and to prove to me that Kodakarajima did not exist he took down a huge tome from the shelf behind him. Its contents covered the entire country. He was right. Kodakarajima wasn't there. And I was glad. Once such a place comes into existence, it usually gets spoiled *out* of existence. I hope that little island and its people survive as they are for as long as it suits them. And by not existing to the rest of the world, they have a far better chance.

The clerk solemnly returned the Post Office book to its shelf and suggested I ask the crew of the boat I'd just left if they would take it when they went back, the post office couldn't. So I did, and they did. Postage free of course, for who was there to stamp it?

From an early age Joan Baxter's interests were travel, dance and writing. She had little schooling though what she did have was good. Joan particularly enjoyed her second school, the result of passing the eleven plus, but sadly was not allowed to finish.

Travelling for ten years, the people met and the experiences shared were memorable. In writing *One Man's Gold* Joan wanted to keep them that way, without embellishment. Glimpses of life, not stories.

Joan Baxter has had two contributions published in Readers Digest, one in a poetry anthology. Her last in the *Oxford International Women's Festival Poetry Anthology*. She has been a frequent contributor to Yoga magazines and her last book, *Sword of No Blade*, published by Samuel Weiser Inc. has been published in Korean in South Korea and in Portuguese in Brazil as well as English speaking countries. For women's activities in self-defence, Joan was interviewed on Radio 4's You and Yours. She also interviewed in Singapore with Peter, Paul and Mary on Singapore Roundup.

Joan worked her own act here in the UK and abroad, plus TV and films in Japan when a foreign face was needed. At home, she was one of a touring company of four, operating 12"-15" high, period-dressed stringed puppets, for the Heap Miniature Theatre.